Shattering t[

Bri

Acknowledgments

The following folks patiently helped me edit, rethink, reconstruct, reformat, and reword this book. Their inputs improved my thinking and writing skills as they provided helpful calibrations that I know will benefit all of my readers:

Dr. Chuck Bagby
Richard Barnett
Brenda Blanchard
Dr. Debbie Byrd
Virginia Harris
Dr. John Lovitt
Dr. Michael Miller
Dr. Phillip Williams

Art Blajos and Eddie Diaz, thank you for allowing me to share your testimonies with my readers.

Copyright, Trademark, and Legal Notices

Preface

Religion: people love it, hate it, disagree about it, and kill over it.

"Church," "religion," and "Jesus" often appear so tightly bundled, that when church people fail, *God Himself* seems hypocritical. However, human doctrines and religious practices often insulate us from the *One* they're supposed to introduce us to.

Even if you're one of the few who haven't been victimized by church hypocrites, could you truthfully say church fulfills your spiritual thirst? Maybe the God of the Bible is looking for something different from us than adhering to religious routines.

Many of us inherit our spiritual beliefs without investigating the truth claims of our religious institutions. Historic writings preserved in the Bible become hopelessly blended into a sea of religious traditions dating back hundreds or thousands of years.

When religious systems unite with culture, and collaborate with personal spiritual preferences, they create caricatures of Christ that may no longer reflect biblical truth. These mental caricatures exaggerate or diminish Jesus' character and core message. As a result, many accept the wrong Jesus, or reject the real one.

Many church-going Christians believe they know the biblical Jesus when they've merely inherited or developed a spiritual sounding blend of tradition, religious practices, routines, rituals, and human doctrines.

Jesus' gospel has often been replaced by Church, culture, and personal preferences that create beautiful stained glass barriers that filters our impressions of the Resurrected Christ.

The next few pages can help you test how much, or how little, some of your beliefs about the Jesus of the Bible may have been shifted. As truth illuminates and exposes our false impressions, barriers to God are shattered.

Let's start shattering some of those stained glass barriers now!

This first edition of *Shattering the Stained Glass Jesus* is dedicated
to the memory of my cousin Tim Sheldon:
loving husband and father,
son, brother, and
friend to all!

Table of Contents

Chapter 1: Breaking Barriers to God

Chapter 2: Where Do You Stand with God?

Chapter 3: What is Truth?

Chapter 4: Defeating Deception

Chapter 5: Why Trust the Bible?

Chapter 6: Caricatures of Christ

Chapter 7: Is Jesus God?

Chapter 8: When God Gets Personal

Appendix A

Chapter 1
Breaking Barriers to God

Therefore, if anyone is in Christ, he is a new creation; old things have passed away; behold, all things have become new. (2 Corinthians 5:17, KJV)

The former Mexican Mafia assassin, Art Blajos, washed cars with other men from similar criminal backgrounds. God changed their lives in dramatic ways and they were now earning money to support the recovery facility they called home; murder and robbery no longer fit their lifestyles.

Although Art knew God transformed his life, he also understood the price. His old gang would hunt him down and test him with a life-or-death decision.

The dreaded day arrived sooner than Art expected.

As the car wash traffic slowed down, Art took a break. Suddenly, a dark sedan, that seemed to come from nowhere, quickly rolled up and stopped next to him. The car window powered down, and a plume of cigar smoke drifted into Art's face. The driver puffed on his cigar again, and demanded in Spanish, "Conejo, what's up?" The driver's question seemed simple on the surface, but it harbored the life-or-death ultimatum Art feared.

Art looked for escape routes but found none. Blajos' carwash colleagues chatted twenty feet away and were oblivious to Art's looming death. Art could return to his gang and live, or die while remaining faithful to the Savior who rescued him from death row and gave him eternal life.

Art quickly and silently prayed, Lord Jesus, if you want to use me and my life, you'll have to do something. All I have to defend myself is this rag in my hand.

Blajos prepared to die as he replied, "I'm not going back with you. Christ changed me, and I live at Victory Outreach now."

After Art prayed, he braced himself for bullets from guns that didn't fire. Instead, puzzled looks overcame the two men in the sedan; after glancing at each other they simply drove away.

While I interviewed Art for this chapter introduction, I asked him if he believed they were supposed to take him dead or alive. Art answered, When they said, 'Conejo, what's up?' they wanted to know if what they heard was true—that I wasn't coming back. They were also giving me a chance to return with them, but if I didn't go back, I believe they were supposed to kill me.

In his book, *Blood In, Blood Out*,[1] Art explains how God reached him on death row, transformed his life, released him from prison, and used him as an evangelist.

Blajos was not looking for God, but God was looking for him. Art's legal challenge overturned his death penalty as prison overcrowding, combined with Art's transformed character, contributed to his early release. Blajos grew in Christian character as he learned about Jesus, the Bible, and prayer, during his stay in a Victory Outreach International recovery home.

Art was not a religious person, and had not been seeking God. About two thousand years before Jesus transformed Art, He transformed another type of assassin. An ultra-religious man who zealously persecuted men, women, and children for the sake of Judaism, encountered the Living God.

> *As he was approaching Damascus on this mission, a light from heaven suddenly shone down around him. He fell to the ground and heard a voice saying to him, 'Saul! Saul! Why are you persecuting me?'*
> *'Who are you, Lord?' Saul asked.*
> *And the voice replied, 'I am Jesus, the one you are persecuting!'*[2]

[1] Art Blajos, *Blood In, Blood Out*, Monarch Books; 1st edition (September 20, 1996)

[2] Acts 9:3-5, NLT

7

We know Saul today as the Apostle Paul, who the Holy Spirit inspired to pen more of the New Testament than any other biblical writer. Saul's collision with the Living Christ turned his life inside out.

Whereas God reached a Mafia assassin *without religion*, He reached Saul of Tarsus *in spite of his religion*.

Like many zealous religious people, Saul served his traditions without knowing the true God. Spiritual blinders fell from Saul's eyes like scales, and all things became new for him.[3]

> If sleeping in garages doesn't turn us into cars, why would attending church make us right with God?

Have all things become new for you or has church become a boring ritual?

Many believe church attendance makes them right with God. Suppose God wants something different from us—like a personal relationshiip?

If sleeping in garages doesn't turn us into cars, why would attending church make us right with God? It didn't make Saul right with God.

My previous motive for attending church didn't include worshiping God. I believed He merely wanted me to spend an hour at church every Sunday and some angel would punch my attendance card—if you were God, would church attendance alone thrill you? I later realized God wanted my heart and I had not given it to Him. Like Saul, my religious traditions blinded me to God's voice, and I didn't believe I could know Him personally this side of Heaven.

For most of my life, I thought Heaven came through "good" works. I didn't know how many works I had to do, or how well I had to do them. Under my good-works-earn-Heaven system, I could easily have missed Heaven by one good work, or by not performing one work correctly.

---

[3] Acts 9:18

Besides, church scandals, hypocritical Christians, and religious people left me with a bad taste in my spiritual mouth for God because. After studying the Bible, I discovered Jesus, like most of us, also detested hypocrites.

> *Hypocrites! Well did Isaiah prophesy about you, saying:*
> > *These people draw near to Me with their mouth*
> > *And honor me with their lips,*
> > *But their heart is far from Me.*
> > *And in vain they worship Me,*
> > *teaching as doctrines the commandments of*
> > *men.*[4]

Jesus doesn't desire hypocritical lip service—He longs for our hearts. What surprised me was how religion had blinded me to some simple biblical truths.

Worldly desires, spiritual deception, and culture create stained glass filters over our spiritual eyes. These alluring filters blind us to the True Living Christ and cause us to create the Jesus we either *want* to see, or want to avoid.

Fortunately, we can easily measure how much—or little—our spiritual filters eclipse our view of the biblical Christ. Are you ready to expose and shatter some stained glass religious perceptions? If so, answer the following questions. According to the Bible;

1. If I believe in God, I will go to Heaven   T   F
2. I will go to Heaven if I am a good person   T   F
3. If I keep the Ten Commandments, I'll go to Heaven   T   F
4. Many paths lead to God   T   F
5. Most people are good at heart   T   F
6. Most people will go to Heaven   T   F
7. God helps those who help themselves   T   F
8. Jesus was a good man, but not God   T   F
9. Hell is not a literal place.   T   F
10. We are all God's children   T   F

---

[4] Matthew 15:7-9

The Bible scores each of these statements as false!

You can find the verses that score this quiz in Appendix A. Most who have not studied the Bible for themselves will score 40% or less. Some grow angry when they discover what they believed *about* the Bible differs from what the Bible actually says.

As I discussed some of the quiz verses with a friend, he raised his voice and said, "That's not the Jesus I grew up with!" His response surprised me until I remembered I felt the same way when the Jesus of my religious perceptions didn't match the Jesus of Scripture.

The bottom line: if we could be wrong about what the God of the Bible says it *doesn't* take to attain Heaven, could we be wrong about what He says *it does take* to go to go there?

Many professing Christians I know cannot explain the Gospel (Good News) of Salvation, why they need it, or how to receive it. Can you?

If you want to let the Bible answer some eye-opening, eternity-shaping questions about Jesus' core message, read on.

Pure and genuine religion in the sight of God the Father means caring for orphans and widows in their distress and refusing to let the world corrupt you.
(James 1:27 NLT)

On a brisk Sunday morning, a train with a mysterious cargo rounded a curve before rolling through a small German town. Wheels screeched against cold steel rails as screams echoed from the train's boxcars.

The train sounded its whistle before rumbling through the small town. The train raced through several more neighborhoods before click-clacking by a church that gathered for their Sunday celebration. The congregant's singing grew much louder to drown out the screams coming from the train.

People were crammed so tightly into the boxcars, that some struggled to breathe. Some died before they reached their destination, yet, they may have been the fortunate ones. This train would deliver its surviving cargo to a Nazi death camp.

A former member of that little church recalled, "If some of the screams reached our ears, we'd just sing a little louder until we could hear them no more. Years have passed, and no one talks about it much anymore, but I still hear that train whistle in my sleep. I can still hear them crying out for help. God forgive all of us who called ourselves Christians, yet did nothing to intervene."[5]

---

[5] "Sing a Little Louder," Repent America, http://www.repentamerica.com/singalittlelouder.html, (13 July 2015)

The Holocaust tragically defined the capacity for evil within human hearts. Jesus provided a remedy for evil that often escapes regular church-going people.

Many traditional religious systems, in conjunction with our culture, have corrupted our impression of Jesus and His core message. For example, as you hear or read, "Jesus," what first pops into your mind?

Hypocrites? Boredom? Religion? A baby in a manger? Christmas trees and ornaments?

Many automatically associate Jesus with a church, religion or church people, but the Bible portrays Him as Savior, Lord, and friend.[6]

Jesus has become almost irrelevant to our culture. The first-century Church of Laodicea was occupied with worldly pursuits and locked Jesus out.

Look! I stand at the door and knock. If you hear my voice and open the door, I will come in, and we will share a meal together as friends.[7]

Why did *Laodicea* lock Jesus out? Their spiritual temperature cooled to lukewarm. The Resurrected Jesus confronts and corrects them;

I know all the things you do, that you are neither hot nor cold. I wish that you were one or the other! But since you are like lukewarm water, neither hot nor cold, I will spit you out of my mouth! You say, 'I am rich. I have everything I want. I don't need a thing!' And you don't realize that you are wretched and miserable and poor and blind and naked.[8]

---

[6] See 1 John 4:14, Luke 6:46, and John 15:14-15

[7] Revelation 3:20 NLT

[8] Revelation 3:15-17 NLT

Laodicea forgot Jesus and His Gospel of Salvation. Have you or your church become spiritually lukewarm?

What is the Gospel of Salvation?

Gospel means good message or good news. However, we can easily lose track of the simplicity of Jesus' Gospel. The Holy Spirit, writing through the Apostle Paul, declares the Gospel of Salvation—the Good News.

Moreover, brethren, I declare to you the gospel which I preached to you, which also you received and in which you stand, by which also you are saved, if you hold fast that word which I preached to you—unless you believed in vain. For I delivered to you first of all that which I also received: that Christ died for our sins according to the Scriptures, and that He was buried, and that He rose again the third day according to the Scriptures, and that He was seen by Cephas, then by the twelve. After that He was seen by over five hundred brethren at once . . . [9]

Notice from this passage that Jesus died, "according to the scriptures." Prophetic writings faithfully predicted and recorded details of His death, burial, and resurrection thousands of years, in advance.

Although most Christians may rightly recognize the Gospel in Easter stories and dramas, few understand their *need* for it. Many believe that Jesus came to make good people better. Suppose instead, Jesus came so that dead souls could *live*?

Why do we need the Gospel?

For decades, I believed I deserved Heaven because I earned it. I attended church and considered myself a good person. I

---

[9] 1 Corinthians 15:1-6

believed that as long as my good deeds outweighed my bad, and as long as I followed most of my church's teachings, I would survive Judgment Day.

I believed good works caused my salvation. I failed to understand that although my good works might be a symptom of right standing with God, they couldn't initiate or cause me to be right with Him.

Besides, by falsely assuming my good works earned Heaven, I could miss Heaven by one good work, or by not performing one or more good works well enough.

I did not read the Bible so I was unaware that the God of the Bible regarded my best works as "filthy rags."

We are all infected and impure with sin.
When we display our righteous deeds,
they are nothing but filthy rags.
Like autumn leaves, we wither and fall,
and our sins sweep us away like the wind.[10]

I failed to understand that if I broke just one of God's Commandments once, I disqualified myself from Heaven.

For the person who keeps all of the laws except one is as guilty as a person who has broken all of God's laws. For the same God who said, "You must not commit adultery," also said, "You must not murder." So if you murder someone but do not commit adultery, you have still broken the law.[11]

Although it's too late for any of us to obey the Ten Commandments perfectly, they serve as guardians and teachers that will lead us to the end of ourselves and teach us about our need for the Savior.

---

[10] Isaiah 64:6-8, NLT

[11] James 2:10-11 NLT

Let me put it another way. The law was our guardian until Christ came; it protected us until we could be made right with God through faith. And now that the way of faith has come, we no longer need the law as our guardian.[12]

Another flaw with my salvation theory hinged on my misunderstandings of grace and faith. I knew they sounded good, but I didn't know they were crucial for my salvation.

For by grace you have been saved through faith, and that not of yourselves; it is the gift of God, not of works, lest anyone should boast.[13]

What do we need to do when we've been presented a gift? Receive it. Nicodemus, a first-century ultra-religious Jewish teacher, came to Jesus at night to ask what he needed to do to be saved.

Jesus answered and said to him,"Are you the teacher of Israel, and do not know these things? Most assuredly, I say to you, We speak what We know and testify what We have seen, and you do not receive Our witness. If I have told you earthly things and you do not believe, how will you believe if I tell you heavenly things? No one has ascended to heaven but He who came down from heaven, that is, the Son of Man who is in heaven. And as Moses lifted up the serpent in the wilderness, even so must the Son of Man be lifted up, that whoever believes in Him should not perish but have eternal life. For God so loved the world that He gave His only begotten Son, that whoever believes in Him should

---

[12] Galatians 3:24-25

[13] Ephesians 2:8-9

*not perish but have everlasting life. For God did not
send His Son into the world to condemn the world,
but that the world through Him might be saved."[14]*

I attended church for forty-some years before someone
explained the Gospel of Salvation to me. I trusted my own corrupt
deeds instead of His completed work on the cross. I relied on
religion as my mediator instead of recognizing the One True
Mediator,[15] Jesus Christ.

Jesus is great news for us and He provides our salvation, but
there is one catch; we need to receive Jesus on His terms, and
not our own.

How Do We Receive Jesus' Salvation?

Many presume, since they believe in God, they will be saved
on Judgment Day. Why do so many assume they're saved
because they believe in God? Even Satan believes in God—and
trembles![16]

God requires something more of us than simply believing He
exists; He wants us to receive Him through the free will He has
given each of us; He will not force us to receive Him.

*If you confess with your mouth the Lord Jesus and
believe in your heart that God has raised Him from the
dead, you will be saved. For with the heart one believes
unto righteousness, and with the mouth confession is
made unto salvation.[17]*

Is Jesus alive in your heart, or is He a religious artifact in your
mind? If you want to surrender your life to Christ, you might pray
something like this from your heart:

---

[14] John 3:3-17

[15] See 1 Timothy 2:5

[16] See James 2:19

[17] Romans 10:9-10

16

Lord Jesus, I receive you by faith and with my heart. I want to make you the Lord of my life. Although I've sinned many times, you suffered and died on the cross to pay for each sin. I receive your sacrifice now for the forgiveness of my sins. I want to know you personally. As I surrender my life to you, please make yourself real to me. Open my heart, mind, soul, and spirit to your voice so that I may hear and obey you.

You may already have peace with God, but is he the God of the Bible or a god of religion? Perhaps he became a god of personal preference? Receiving the right God, the right way matters to Him.

Do You Stand with the God of the Bible?

If someone asked me twenty-five years ago if I was going to Heaven, I would have answered, "I hope so." What I really would have meant is, I didn't know. After studying the Bible, I realized I could know if I was Heaven-bound or not.[18] Do you know for certain where you will spend eternity? The following figure may help you quickly identify where you might stand with the God of the Bible.

Figure 2.1's opening question asks, "Do you believe God exists?" Most believe God exists, and we explored how even Satan believes in God—and trembles! Mere intellectual belief provides no benefit, but we need to accept God's existence before knowing if our theologies align with the God of the Bible.

Similarly, Psalm 53:1 argues against atheism and claims that fools say in their hearts that there is no God. Romans 1:20 further expounds that since God's creation reveals the Godhead, we have no excuse since we can know the God of the Bible exists.

Let's presume you believe God exists as we proceed to the next question, "Is Jesus the only way to God?" This question encompasses the most contentious issues in the world. This

---

[18] 1 John 5:13

crucial question divides cultures, religions, denominations, friends, and families. In your view, Is Jesus is the only way to God?

I believed Jesus was my way to God, but I also believed others could reach God in other ways. I hadn't considered that multiple ways to God negated Jesus' purpose. If other ways to God exist, then Jesus died in vain, and Jesus was either lying, deceived, or delusional when He claimed, "I am the way the truth, and the life. No one comes to the Father except through Me."

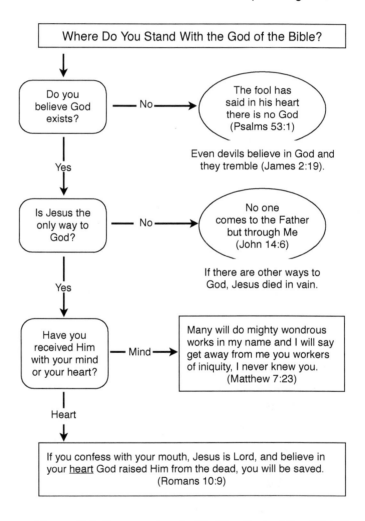

Figure 2.1. Do you stand with The God of the Bible?

18

Lying, deceived, delusional people might get themselves crucified, but they can't fulfill thousands of years worth of hundreds of Bible prophecies about Jesus' birth, life, and crucifixion. Also, delusional people cannot raise themselves from the dead.

During His crucifixion, Jesus could have been freed merely by asking His Father for legions of angels to rescue Him. He refused any angelic support and endured excruciating, horrific pain as He paid for our sins.

When Jesus asked His Father for another way to redeem mankind, Jesus' Father provided no other way besides the cruel cross. If there was not another way for Jesus, how could another way exist for us—except through Jesus?

If you believe God exists and that Jesus is the only way to Him, figure 2.1's final question asks, "Have you received Him with your mind or your heart?"

Salvation depends upon our willingness to move Jesus' sacrifice the short distance from our heads to hearts. Religion may provide intellectual knowledge about Jesus, but He knocks at the doors of hearts. [19]

The Bible clearly teaches Jesus is the only way to God and Jesus agrees His way is narrow.

We can certainly disagree with Him or doubt His words, but Jesus does not allow any middle ground. He does not logically allow us to blend His way with any other ways. Jesus is either the only way to God, or He is not a way at all.

Besides, most other religions and beliefs also present themselves as the only way to God. Therefore, we cannot logically bundle biblical Christianity with any other ways. Many prefer to live their own life instead of surrendering it to Christ. They create a complicated, contradictory, politically correct, false universe of ways that lead to Heaven.

Finally, most religions and philosophical systems claim they lead to God but add some form of human effort, additional works, or obedience to certain doctrines. Contrary to many

---

[19] Revelation 3:20

denominational teachings, God does not require any works for admission to Heaven.[20]

> *Christianity is also the only religion that recognizes the hopeless gap between man and a Holy and Righteous God, teaching that salvation can only be obtained through God's grace. All other religions teach that salvation can be achieved through human effort. I think at this point we should be able to agree that the major world religions are quite different, with many conflicting and contradictory views. To hold that all religions are equally true is simply not a rational belief.[21]*

Although many religions devise deeds and prescribe rules for reaching God, the Bible teaches Jesus has already done everything we need to be saved. We can't earn God's salvation, and we can't add to Jesus' perfect, complete sacrifice. He only requires us to believe and receive him on His terms, and His blood will remove our sins.

For many, Jesus' claims may sound too good to be true. Others desire many ways to God (or devise their own gods) and even challenge truth's existence.

Can we know truth exists? Can we really know what is true? How do beliefs differ from truth? If you want solid answers to these deep questions, keep reading.

---

[20] See Ephesians 2:7-9. True believers walk in God's works because of salvation but not to *cause* salvation.

[21] Bible Evidences - Other Religions, http://www.bibleevidences.com/other_rlgns.htm (accessed November 10, 2014).

Chapter 3
What is Truth?

Pilate said, So you are a king?
Jesus responded, You say I am a king. Actually, I was
born and came into the world to testify to the truth. All
who love the truth recognize that what I say is true.
What is truth? Pilate asked. (John 18:37-38)

The briefcase handcuffed to a man's wrist bobbed in the waves as ocean currents nudged the mysterious, waterlogged soldier toward Spanish shores. As Allied radio broadcasts alerted their audience to Major Martin's disappearance, enemy ears also listened attentively to the broadcasts and hoped to find Martin first.

The year was 1943, and as World War II raged, Adolph Hitler understood dead man did tell tales. The Germans found Martin's dead body after it washed ashore near Portugal and quickly analyzed his secrets. Then the Germans reassembled everything and quickly let the Allies "find" Major Martin's corpse and briefcase.

Major Martin delivered the bait—and was the bait—for a deception plan named Operation Mincemeat.

In reality, Martin's body was the corpse of another soldier who died of pneumonia. The Germans would see pneumonia as a cause of death consistent with drowning.

The British submarine, The Seraph, released the body and its deceptive information from a torpedo tube to drift towards the Spanish coast. The Allies hoped they estimated ocean current patterns well enough to float Major Martin into Hitler's waiting hands.

The Allies painted a realistic, yet deceptive picture of one of their officers carrying important, subtly disguised secrets. Like most deceptions, the picture looked true but was not. If Hitler suspected a trap, Operation Mincemeat would fail.

Germany confirmed the anticipated allied invasion of Italy but discovered an unexpected twist after analyzing Martin's information. Instead of invading Sicily, the Allies would apparently seize the less fortified island of Sardinia.

Hitler responded to Martin's secrets by moving forces from Sicily to protect Sardinia. He anticipated surprising and crushing the Allies, but Germany fell prey to an elaborate deception plan and protected the wrong island.

Jesus spoke extensively about truth and said He was born and came into the world to testify to the truth.[22] Truth alone exposes deceptions.

Yet, great deceptions always seem true and cause us to believe or do something we wouldn't do if we only knew the truth.

Major Martin's misleading information seemed authentic enough to cause Hitler to move his defenses and lose Sicily as he gleaned the consequences of acting on his false beliefs.

Unfortunately, many in our culture doubt absolute truth exists and believe individuals create it themselves.

Although truth has been pronounced dead by our postmodern culture, we can restore confidence in it as we distinguish the content of truth (what statements are true) from the concept of truth (what truth is).

The late, great Christian philosopher and thinker, Dr. Francis Schaeffer observed, "What we believe about truth shapes everything about us."

If someone doesn't believe in the concept of truth, they invent their own truth content before mistakenly equating their beliefs with truth.

Deception provides us the most concrete proof truth exists. Two simple questions help us regain lost confidence in truth.

---

[22] John 18:37

1.) Are you absolutely sure someone has ever lied to you?
2.) How did you recognize those lies if the truth didn't expose them?

Can you identify any other way to discover lies except by comparing their claims with the truth? We can't expose lies any other way except through the truth.

If truth is our only ally for exposing lies, why do so many doubt it exists? Jesus teaches mans' fear of having their sins exposed keeps them from embracing the truth.

God's light came into the world, but people loved the darkness more than the light, for their actions were evil. All who do evil hate the light and refuse to go near it for fear their sins will be exposed. But those who do what is right come to the light so others can see that they are doing what God wants. [23]

As many in our culture try to escape the Light, they equate "belief" with "truth" and then pretend "belief" doesn't exist. As a result, we may hear conversations like, "My truth is that all ways lead to God, what's your truth?" If people who ask, "What's your truth," understood the differences between truth and belief, they would ask, "I believe all ways lead to God, what do you believe?"

Beliefs or Truth?

It may be helpful to look up "belief" and "truth" in your own dictionary and note the differences. I'll use the following two definitions help clarify differences between truth and belief:

Truth: Conformity to fact or reality; exact accordance with that which is, or has been, or shall be. [24]

---

[23] John 3:19-21, New Living Translation

[24] TRUTH - Definition from the KJV Dictionary, http://av1611.com/kjbp/kjv-dictionary/truth.html (accessed October 23, 2014)

Belief: A persuasion of the truth, or an assent of mind to the truth of a declaration, proposition or alleged fact, on the ground of evidence, distinct from personal knowledge.[25]

Notice how truth conforms with fact or reality whereas belief expresses how *persuaded* we are of that truth. True beliefs align with the truth: false beliefs do not.

Although the truth may persuade us to change our beliefs, truth is unaffected by our beliefs. Beliefs may clash over what is true, but they cannot cause or change the truth.

If your car ran out of gas and you broke open the fuel gage and manually moved the needle from "E" to "F," would gas fill your tank? Of course not. Fuel gages reflect gasoline levels (truth), but they do not add or remove gas. The truth reflected by our gages may cause us to purchase gas, or endure the consequences of walking to a gas station. Can we apply this truth/belief distinction to God?

> Truth is true even if no one believes it, and lies are false even if everyone believes them.

Some skeptics doubt God exists because they can't see Him. However, these same skeptics rarely challenge the existence of radio waves, x-rays, gravity, atomic particles, or other non-tangible scientific truths.

Truth is true even if no one believes it, and lies are false even if everyone believes them. For example, a few hundred years ago most believed the earth was flat. As mathematics, geometry, astronomy, satellites, and manned spacecraft gathered facts about Earth's shape, the world's beliefs began aligning with the true shape of our planet. While most believed the earth was flat, it remained spherical as it revolved around the sun and rotated on its axis unaffected by the majority's beliefs.

---

[25] BELIEF - Definition from the KJV Dictionary, http://av1611.com/kjbp/kjv-dictionary/belief.html (accessed October 23, 2014)

Just as science and history help us reconstruct the facts about the earth's true shape, they help us investigate other truth claims.

Many don't want to believe recorded history surrounding Jesus' life, death, burial, and resurrection. The Bible paints a consistent, uniform picture of a supernatural Jesus, who came to deliver us from our sins. His miracles provide overwhelming evidence that Jesus is the one prophesied in the Old Testament.

The Apostle John explains his motive for writing his letter.

> *These things I have written to you who believe in the name of the Son of God, that you may know that you have eternal life, and that you may continue to believe in the name of the Son of God.[26]*

The Bible teaches many will call Jesus "Lord," and perform miracles in His name, but will be surprised at Jesus' response to them on Judgment Day.

> *Not everyone who says to Me, 'Lord, Lord,' shall enter the kingdom of heaven, but he who does the will of My Father in heaven. Many will say to Me in that day, 'Lord, Lord, have we not prophesied in Your name, cast out demons in Your name, and done many wonders in Your name?' And then I will declare to them, 'I never knew you; depart from Me, you who practice lawlessness!'[27]*

Although the wonder-working, demon-defying prophets delivered many mighty works in Jesus' name, they never knew Jesus or received His truth.

What Do You Believe About Truth?

---

[26] 1 John 5:13

[27] Matthew 7:21-23

"How does your generation view truth?" I asked my 20-something waitress.

"We sort of feel that truth is what's true for the individual—there's no absolutes," she answered.

"How would you feel if you worked forty hours but got paid for twenty," I continued, "because your bosses' truth was that you only worked twenty?"

She thought a moment and slowly responded, "I guess some truths are absolute."

Exactly! Some truths are absolute—and they may deliver painful, often irreversible consequences, if we don't believe them. Mistaken paychecks or burns from hot stoves snap us out of philosophical preferences and back into reality.

Unfortunately, many arbitrarily redefine truth with their feelings.

In his article, "Americans Are Most Likely to Base Truth on Feelings," George Barna, founder of a leading marketing research firm focused on the intersection of faith and culture, asked teenagers in two separate national surveys if morality was absolute, or relative. 83% of these teens believed truth was relative to their circumstances; 64% of adults claimed truth is always relative to the person or their situation.[28] Barna's survey illustrates growing skepticism about absolute truth's existence. Increasing numbers believe all truth is relative.

Relativists often evaluate truth claims with their feelings or preferences, whereas absolutists discern truth with their minds. Relativists may ask, "What's your truth?" whereas absolutists ask, "What is true?"

Jesus is an absolutist because when He said, "I am the way, the truth, and the life, and no one comes to the Father but through Me," He declared war on all other beliefs espousing other ways to God. In the following passage, Jesus defines HIs purpose on the earth in terms of truth.

---

[28]*Americans are Most Likely to Base Truth on Feelings*, Barna Group, https://www.barna.org/barna-update/article/5-barna-update/67-americans-are-most-likely-to-base-truth-on-feelings#.VaR81nht7Zc, Accessed 13 July 2015

I was born and entered the world so that I could bear witness to the truth. Everyone who cares for truth, who has any feeling for the truth, recognizes my voice . . . [29]

If Jesus was a relativist, He might have said,

I was born and entered the world so that I could bear witness to whatever people want to be true. Everyone who cares for what is true for them, who has any feeling for whatever they want truth to be, recognizes my voice or someone else's voice, it really doesn't matter . . .

Yes, truth *does* matter, because if Jesus is the *only* way to God, no one can go to Heaven any other way. Jesus as the only way means *all* other ways to God are *wrong.*

We are certainly free to *disbelieve* the Jesus of the Bible, but we can't logically *blend* his absolutes with opposite beliefs. For example, Jesus can't be the *only* way to God, and merely *one of many ways* to Him.

A stanza from Steve Turner's poem, *Creed,* illustrates the insanity of blending Jesus' truth claims with other beliefs:

We believe that all religions are basically the same
at least the one that we read was.
They all believe in love and goodness.
They only differ on matters of creation,
sin, heaven, hell, God, and salvation. [30]

Do you believe what the God of the Bible says about creation, sin, Heaven, Hell, and salvation? Many don't believe the truth because they believed the deception offered by worldly philosophies and false doctrines. The Bible warns;

---

[29] See John 18:37

[30] Poem: *Creed,* by Steve Turner - PoemHunter.com, http://www.poemhunter.com/poem/creed/ (accessed October 24, 2014).

Beware lest anyone cheat you through philosophy and empty deceit, according to the tradition of men, according to the basic principles of the world, and not according to Christ. [31]

To void the truth, our culture often teaches that we can blend opposing truth claims and avoid negative consequences, but we can't. We examined, for example that my waitress changed her view of truth when the truth became personal and mattered to her bank account.

> When ten religions teach opposite, and contradictory ways to God, these ten ways to God might all be wrong, but they can't all logically be right.

Similarly, Jesus can't be the only way to God and also one of the many ways to Him. The "all paths lead to God" philosophy fails for another often-overlooked reason.

The alleged bundle of many ways that supposedly lead to God contains religions that also claim they're the only way to God. When ten religions teach opposite, and contradictory ways to God, these ten ways to God might all be wrong, but they can't all logically be right.

Anti-truth strategies falsely assure people they can deny what is true by questioning truth's existence. Deep down, even the most devout truth skeptics know absolute truth exists. Do you believe in absolute truth? Here are a few examples to ponder:

- *Belief* and *truth* are different words.
- We spell *belief* and *truth* differently.
- *Belief* and *truth* have different definitions.
- People disagree about absolute truth itself.
- We are all aging.

---

[31] Colossians 2:8

- We have each lied.
- Others have lied to us.

Finally, if you still doubt absolute truth exists, ask yourself, "When I know I've been deceived, how did I know I was lied to, if the truth didn't expose the lies?"

Truth Fountains

I've found it helpful to envision truth as an explosion of facts radiating from reality. These facts stream from touching a hot stove, crime scenes, car accidents, or historical events like Jesus' resurrection from the dead.

When we reconstruct historical events from facts, we complete a picture that answers, who, what, when, where, why, and how? The Bible and other historical, archaeological, linguistic, academic, prophetic, and scientific evidence help us reassemble a picture of the Historical Jesus and His Gospel of Salvation.

Many do not believe the fact of Jesus' resurrection and their beliefs will shift the moment they die. Delayed consequences often provide the illusion that we can deny or reframe the truth with no repercussions. Other facts cause us to respond properly or endure immediate responses.

Imagine, for example, a robber holds a gun to your head and demands, "Your money or your life?" What would you do in this situation? Even if you are a truth skeptic, you are probably not skeptical enough to sacrifice your life.

We may not often think about it, but our ability to live another day often depends upon our ability to navigate facts and truths. When we drive our cars, for example, we rapidly process the information coming to our senses and continually adjust our speed, react to other vehicles, change lanes, avoid guardrails, and respond to car horns and traffic signals. Failure to properly respond to sensory facts lead to death or dents.

If wrong physical decisions result in physical consequences, why wouldn't wrong spiritual decisions result in painful, eternal, spiritual consequences? They certainly will. Although time and space separate us from Jesus' resurrection, the physical evidence remains. How do we obtain truth?

Imagine a mother warns her child, "The stove is hot—don't touch it, or you'll burn yourself!" She makes a truth claim and warns of consequences. If a child disregards his mother's warning, consequences follow confirming or denying mom's truth claims.

Statements like this mother's warning are sometimes called propositional truths; they describe reality through words and language. True statements correspond to reality, and false ones do not.

TRUTH STATEMENTS: Language About Stoves

"The stove is hot! Don't touch it or you'll burn yourself!"

TRUTH EXPERIENCES: Touching Stoves

"My skin blistered after touching that hot stove!"

TRUTH EXPERIMENTS: Researching Stoves

"A thermometer reads this stove's temperature as 212 degrees Fahrenheit."

TRUTH REASONING :Thinking About Stoves

"This stove boils water, therefore, the stove must be hot!"

Figure 3.1. Four Fountains of Truth

Our experiences also reveal the truth. As we revisit our stove example, suppose the child ignores his mother's warning and touches the stove. If the stove is hot enough, the child immediately experiences pain and burned skin.

A third way to determine the stove's temperature is by experimenting with it. Scientific instruments extend our senses and provide facts and truth about the universe, atoms, and stoves. Suppose a thermometer measures the stove temperature as 212-degrees Fahrenheit. This temperature reading indicates the stove is hot enough to boil water, cook food, or burn our skin.

Finally, we obtain truth by experimenting with reality. As we create and test theories, new knowledge emerges and often shows us what we can expect in the future.

Suppose we see water boiling above a stove burner. We would rightly reason, based upon past experiences, if the stove boils water, it's hot enough to burn me.

Although we may not know certain truths *exactly*, we can know some truths well enough to choose properly and avoid painful consequences.

Descartes answered a question that haunted philosophers for many years, "How do I know I exist?" Descartes, after much thought answered, "I think, therefore, I am." [32]

Some skeptics still argue against the truth and claim, "Since we cannot know the truth precisely, how can we know the truth at all?" How well do we need to know a stove's temperature to safely cook safely with it?

After all, billions of people worldwide cooked food today without getting burned but not one of them knew the *exact* temperature of their stove. Some knew their stove's temperature within a degree or two, but not within a millionth, billionth, or a trillionth of a degree.

Although we may not know certain truths exactly, we can know some truths well enough to choose properly and avoid painful consequences. Knowing the truth also helps us avoid pain, injury, premature death, and eternal torment.

Relative Truth? Absolutely!

Relative means *in relation to something else*. Thus, our universe contains many relative truths. Every atom in the universe

---

[32] *Discourse on the Method*, Part IV (1637 – written in French but with inclusion of "*Cogito ergo sum*") and §7 of part I of *Principles of Philosophy* (1644 – written in Latin).

is relative to every other atom; each star and planet in the universe continuously changes in distance relative to every other planet and star.

Albert Einstein published his theory of relativity in 1916 and used it to explain the interrelationships between matter and energy. Einstein's theory applies to light, planets, stars, and galaxies but also explains why so many things that appear stationary on the earth move at incredible speeds relative to other objects.[33]

Someone who appears to be standing still on Earth's equator travels approximately 1000 miles per hour (mph) with earth's rotation. In addition, our planet orbits the sun at 66,000 mph. Additionally, our solar system moves around the center of our galaxy at about 483,000 mph.[34]

Therefore, someone who appears motionless as they stand on the equator is actually moving hundreds of thousands of miles per hour relative to an observer from beyond our solar system. Meanwhile, back on Earth, people walk, drive, or fly at speeds relative to other people, places, and things.

Despite all of these relative truths, Einstein cautioned that relativity applies only to physics, and not to ethics. He rightly anticipated moral calamity, social decay, and confusion if society started substituting relative truths for God's absolutes.

Consider millions of people who purchase all of the tickets in a lottery. On the day of the drawing, millions of pieces of worthless lottery tickets are thrown away as their value plummets to zero. One piece of formerly worthless paper, however, skyrockets in value to millions of dollars because it matches the most important absolute truth of the lottery: the winning number.

Although each purchased number set is still relative to every other number set, only the one number set that absolutely and completely matches the winning number qualifies for money.

Many gamble on lotteries but many more gamble with their endless destiny because they don't know for certain if they have eternal life or not.

---

[33] space.com, accessed 15 June 2015

[34] www.astrosociety.org, accessed 15 June 2015

The Apostle John disagrees and might say no one has to gamble with their salvation:

These things I have written to you who believe in the name of the Son of God, that you may know that you have eternal life, and that you may continue to believe in the name of the Son of God. [35]

If God's spiritual, absolute truths don't exist, Jesus wasted His life because He said, He came into the world to testify to the truth.[36] Why would Jesus claim to be the truth, testify to the truth, and die for it, if we couldn't know the truth?

Father God is not cruel, and Jesus is not a fool. The Bible teaches salvation comes only through Jesus is the way and no other ways exist to God.

Some never receive Christ because they believe His one road to God seems narrow and unfair. However, God loves and provides salvation for each of us who receive Him on His terms and not our own.

For the wrath of God is revealed from heaven against all ungodliness and unrighteousness of men, who suppress the truth in unrighteousness, because what may be known of God is manifest in them, for God has shown it to them. For since the creation of the world His invisible attributes are clearly seen, being understood by the things that are made, even His eternal power and Godhead, so that they are without excuse, because, although they knew God, they did not glorify Him as God, nor were thankful, but became futile in their thoughts, and their foolish hearts were darkened. [37]

---

[35] 1 John 5:13

[36] John 18:37

[37] Romans 1:18-21

33

Mark Twain observed, "A lie can travel halfway around the world while the truth is putting on its shoes."[38]

I imagine Twain could never envision a lie that challenges truth's existence.

Anti-truth is a strategy that denies the existence of objective, absolute truth. It replaces moral absolutes with the notion of "personal truths." Anti-truth promises people that their beliefs form truth. Anti-truth ignores powerful linkages between truth and consequences.

Physical truths deliver their consequences almost immediately (touch a hot stove—burn your skin) and force us to align our beliefs with the truth or pay an immediate, often painful price.

Traditional deception attacks the things that *are true*, but anti-truth attacks objective truth *itself*. Anti-truth discourages us from thinking about information as true or false and encourages us to combine, consolidate, and blend beliefs.

A favorite anti-truth strategy tries to "synthesize" the concept of absolute truth out of existence by allowing people to believe they alone determine truth; unfortunately, synthesis hides the consequences.

Synthesis is just a fancy word for rationalizing or believing whatever we want by trying to merge even contradictory truth claims (i.e. Jesus the only way to God *and* He is one of many ways to God). Dr. Francis Schaeffer describes synthesis:

Instead of antithesis (some things are true and their opposite untrue), truth and moral rightness will be found in the flow of history, a synthesis of them . . . Today, not only in philosophy but in politics, government, and individual morality, our generation sees solutions in terms of synthesis and not absolutes.

---

[38] Mark Twain: *A lie can travel...*, http://www.quotationspage.com/quote/23633.html (accessed October 24, 2014).

When this happens, truth, as people had always thought of truth, has died.[39]

Truth hasn't really died, but synthesis leads many to believe they can invent their own reality. Fortunately, consequences often snap us back into reality as they reinforce the truth. Consequences, for example, remind us that if we touch a hot stove, our fingers burn.

Synthesis often cuts the linkage between beliefs and consequences. Jesus restores our sense of eternal consequences and reminds us that eternal consequences await each of us.

Enter by the narrow gate; for wide is the gate and broad is the way that leads to destruction, and there are many who go in by it. Because narrow is the gate and difficult is the way which leads to life, and there are few who find it.[40]

Moral shortcuts and *broadways* try, but can't compensate for hurt, anger, bitterness, despair, shame, emptiness, guilt, and purposelessness. Many rich, famous, and powerful people live for pleasure. King Solomon didn't withhold himself from life's pleasures either but found them empty.

So I became greater than all who had lived in Jerusalem before me, and my wisdom never failed me. Anything I wanted, I would take. I denied myself no pleasure. I even found great pleasure in hard work, a reward for all my labors. But as I looked at everything I had worked so hard to accomplish, it was all so meaningless—like chasing the wind. There was nothing really worthwhile anywhere.[41]

---

[39] How Then Shall We Live? Dr. Francis Schaeffer, p. 163

[40] Matthew 7:13-14

[41] Ecclesiastes 2:9-11, New Living Translation

Solomon thought he could attain meaning through pleasure and hard work but instead found emptiness. The god of this age blinded Solomon had been blinded by the god of this age that blinds many today:

> But even if our gospel is veiled, it is veiled to those who are perishing, whose minds the god of this age has blinded, who do not believe, lest the light of the gospel of the glory of Christ, who is the image of God, should shine on them. [42]

Truth alone exposes the lies of the god of this age, and all other deceptions. Have you been deceived about truth? Do you understand how belief and truth differ? If you want to defeat deception, read on.

---

[42] 2 Corinthians 4:3-4

Chapter 4
Defeating Deception

Beloved, do not believe every spirit, but test the spirits, whether they are of God; because many false prophets have gone out into the world. (1 John 4:1)

A fire ball blazed through space at nearly 100,000 miles per hour as it trailed thousands of miles of ions and dust. Despite its speed, the twenty-five mile-wide Hale-Bopp comet would be visible for up to nineteen months before disappearing into the depths of space.

As Hale-Bopp stirred the world's curiosity, a group near San Diego, California, monitored the comet as though their lives depended on it—and their lives would depend upon it.

During late March of 1997, Marshall Applewhite led his thirty-eight followers to believe the comet was being chased by a UFO. He convinced them that if they committed suicide at the right time, they would be taken aboard the spacecraft and ushered into better lives. Applewhite and his followers belonged to a cult known as *Heaven's Gate.* Their ages ranged from twenty-six to seventy-two years old, and they believed Applewhite's fables.

The deceived victims covered themselves with purple cloth before poisoning themselves. Authorities discovered the Heaven's Gate members' bodies in beds near packed luggage. They wore matching black tee shirts, sweat pants, and athletic shoes. Each wore an arm band that read, *Heaven's Gate Away Team.* Finally, each cult member had a five-dollar bill and three quarters to pay their alleged intergalactic toll as they traveled with the UFO.

Thirty-eight people believed Applewhite and chose to die for a lie that sounded like the truth to them.

Tragically, Applewhite equipped *Heaven's Gate's* victims with everything they needed for their planned intergalactic travels—except the truth. Applewhite's stories sounded right to his followers, but so do all successful deceptions.

A proverb reminds us; there is a way that seems right to a man, but in the end it leads to death.[43] The Apostle Paul commended Christians who tested the things anyone taught them about the Bible with the Scriptures themselves.

Paul's method works except under one common condition: when we deceive ourselves.

How Do We Deceive Ourselves?

Heaven's Gate believed Applewhite's fables and apparently, so did Applewhite. Like Applewhite and his followers, our desires often shape our perception. We tend to discount facts that conflict with our preferences and embrace lies that reinforce our desires.

When desires drive our perceptions, truth seems clouded and difficult to receive. Figure 4.1 shows how desire-driven perceptions reject the truth or exchange it for lies.

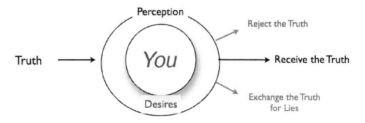

Figure 4.1. When desires drive our perception we tend to reject the truth or exchange it for lies so we can live, feel, and believe what we like, instead of receiving and internalizing what is true.

---

[43] See Proverbs 14:12

Many anorexics, including those who may be dangerously thin and close to death, often perceive themselves as overweight no matter how much contrary evidence exists. Doctors' counsel, measurements, body weight, or the appearance of skin and bones reflected in a mirror fails to change the perceptions of most anorexics.

Pilots do not usually desire to crash their planes but when their perception becomes clouded, and they rely on their feelings instead of the truth. The outcome is fatal. Vertigo and bad weather combine and often cause pilots to ignore their gages and rely on their feelings instead. Consequently, many vertigo-afflicted pilots die as their aircraft spiral into the ground or sea.

Many today suffer from spiritual vertigo or spiritual anorexia. Many spiritual anorexics suffer from symptoms of purposelessness, emptiness, meaninglessness, depression, and despair. Instead of recognizing and receiving spiritual truth, victims of spiritual vertigo/anorexia protect their deadly decisions.

For example, one potential *truth assassin* mailed a bomb to San Antonio Pastor John Hagee. It detonated on a conveyor belt in the Dallas post office without hurting anyone. The FBI eventually caught the bomber and asked him why he did it.

He replied, "When I heard this man preach on television, I knew what he was saying was the absolute truth, and the only way to silence him was to kill him."

Notice that this would-be truth assassin:

1) Recognized and acknowledged the truth

2) Did not want the truth

3) Sought to eliminate the truth

4) Planned a murder to silence truth's voice

Since murdering messengers makes messes and carries prison sentences, many *anti-truth evangelists* focus their effort on killing the *idea* of absolute truth itself.

When we reject the truth or exchange it for lies, we create tension within ourselves that makes us anxious. People sometimes contend with this anxiety by creating intentional blind spots. In *Vital Lies, Simple Truths*, Daniel Goleman explains;

> *The mind can protect itself against anxiety by diminishing awareness. This mechanism produces a blind spot: a zone of blocked attention and self-deception. Such blind spots occur at each major level of behaviour from the psychological to the social.*[44]

Although truth skeptics frequently deny truth and reality, most of them look both ways before crossing busy streets because what *appears* to be a semi-truck may actually *be* one. When we deny reality and clash with it, we receive consequences that produce pain or death (physical or spiritual).

If someone handed you three mushrooms that looked identical and told you two of them were poisonous, would you risk eating *any* of them? Of course not. Unfortunately, we can't usually view the consequence that follow us to our graves so for many, it becomes easier to deny eternal truths and their consequences.

Jesus described a rich man who died and then lived tormented by eternal flames and thirst. The wealthy victim wanted to spare his brothers his horrific fate and reasoned with Abraham, "If someone is sent to them from the dead, then they will repent of their sins and turn to God."

Abraham replied, "If they won't listen to Moses and the prophets, they won't listen even if someone rises from the dead."[45]

How Do Others Deceive Us?

Ultimately, deceivers try to change our beliefs and behaviors so we do something we wouldn't have done, if we had only known the truth.

---

[44] Mike Norman Economics: Self-Deception, Self- Delusion and .., http://mikenormaneconomics.blogspot.com/2012/11/self-deception-self-delusion-and-self.html (accessed October 25, 2014).

[45] See Luke 16:19-31

Deception causes us to believe something that seems true, but is not. Deceptions conceal the real and reveal the false by artfully blending truth with lies. Deceivers twist some truths and suppress others as they try to reshape reality's appearance.

Each of the arrows coming from "Truth" in figure 4.2 represent facts that radiate from truth—from reality. The four arrows that connect "TRUTH" with "DECEPTION" in figure 4.2 represent facts that a deceiver intercepts and manipulates to affect our beliefs.

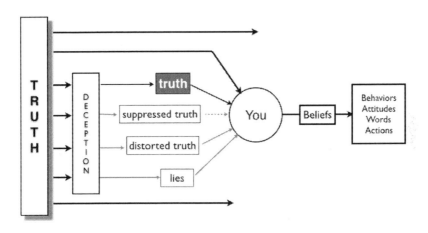

Figure 4.2. Truth radiates facts represented by arrows. Deception releases some facts, as it suppresses or distorts other facts, or injects lies. Countering deception requires we believe in, and independently collect truth that is available to each of us.

Detectives reconstruct crime scenes and collect the facts (represented by arrows) that *radiate* from crimes. As detectives interview eyewitnesses, collect DNA samples, bullets, and other information, they reconstruct the truth that details the crime. Detectives' jobs end when they collect enough facts to reconstruct the truth about the crime.

Many great detective stories show how criminals attempt to deceive and   ingeniously manipulate the truth by creating false

41

pictures of their crimes. They suppress, distort, or lie about the truth. Sometimes, they selectively release facts that create false pictures of their crimes.

In figure 4.2, "DECEPTION" intercepts and modifies the truth before presenting it to "You." Deceivers release some "truth" (shown in the black box) as they suppresses other truths. Deception may also feed us "distorted truth" or present "lies."

The single arrow that connects "TRUTH" with "You" in figure 4.2 represents truth that reaches "You" and could expose the deception.

Ultimately, deceivers try to change our beliefs and behaviors so we do something we wouldn't have done, if we had only known the truth.

Fortunately, facts help us determine the truth and expose lies. The detached arrowheads at the top and bottom of figure 4.2 represent discoverable facts.

Imagine "You" does not believe truth exists. Would he look for facts or believe them when he finds them? Those who deny truth's existence will not search for such facts and will align their beliefs with the deceiver's plan. Once our beliefs change, our behaviors, attitudes, words, and actions change and cause us to swallow the bait.

In the case of spiritual deceptions, we might substitute spirituality or religion for the relationship God wants to have through each of us through Jesus.

If you falsely believed, for example, I'm a good person who deserves Heaven, why would you receive Jesus?[46]

Similarly, if you believed, all paths lead to God, you would likely discount the Jesus of the Bible who proclaims that He alone

---

[46] See Romans 3:23

is the way, the truth, and the life, and that no one comes to the Father but through Him.[47]

Many have difficulty today with the concept of absolute truth and its interplay with deception. Plants, animals, and nature do not share the skeptic's struggle about truth. Many animals routinely rely on deception to trap their prey. As you read the following examples, observe how truth and lies interact and produce consequences.

For example, the sea anemone looks and acts like an edible saltwater plant but in reality, it is a deceptive animal. When a fish swims close enough to nibble on the anemone's leaf like tentacles, the sea anemone stings, paralyzes, and devours its dazed prey.

Clown fish add to the illusion and swim unharmed through the sea anemones' lethal, leaf-like tendrils. Clown fish collaborators benefit by eating scraps left from the anemones' victims.

In another natural deception, bolas spiders hunt by putting a blob of sticky silk on the end of a strong strand of web that forms the bolas. Bolas spiders then bait the silk blob with female moth pheromones. The spider next swings the fragrant bolas and snags male moths drawn to the scented blob. Once a bolas sticks to the moth, the spider merely reels in and devours its prey.

Now the Spirit expressly says that in latter times some will depart from the faith, giving heed to deceiving spirits and doctrines of demons, speaking lies in hypocrisy, having their own conscience seared with a hot iron.[48]

Although many deny absolute truth, others search for it to protect themselves in worldly contracts, business decisions, and relationships. Shouldn't we exercise the same discretion for spiritual matters?

For example, if the truth doesn't exist, many of Jesus' statements become irrelevant. Jesus said, "And you shall know

---

[47] See John 14:6

[48] 1 Timothy 4:1-2

the truth, and the truth shall make you free," (John 8:32). Do you feel free? If not, you may have been deceived about the Bible or what sets it apart from any other spiritual writings. The Bible claims, "All scripture is given by inspiration of God, and is profitable for doctrine, for reproof, for correction, for instruction in righteousness, that the man of God may be complete, thoroughly equipped for every good work," (2 Timothy 3:16-17)

How could the biblical writings prove God inspired them or not? You will find out in the next chapter.

CHAPTER 5
Why Trust the Bible?

Above all, you must understand that no prophecy in Scripture came from the prophets themselves or because they wanted to prophesy. It was the Holy Spirit who moved the prophets to speak from God. (2 Peter 1:20-21, NLT)

A Bedouin boy tended his flock on the Northwest side of the Dead Sea. He cautiously approached a mysterious cave that caught his attention. Perhaps one of his animals strayed into the cave, and if not, he thought, it might still be fun to rout any lurking creatures.

He hurled a rock into the cave. He didn't hear the noise of scurrying creatures, but a strange, shattering sound. He peered through the mouth of the cave and discovered many ancient, sealed pottery containers—including a broken one.

The real value of the shepherd boy's discoveries would not be known for many years as they passed from antiquity dealers to scholars who eventually recognized the genuine value of the shepherd boy's discoveries.

Nearby caves harbored even more of the mysterious scrolls—some dating back before 250 B.C. Ancient librarians sealed copies of most Old Testament books in the clay jars along with other historical writings.

The scrolls constituted one of the greatest archeological discoveries of the twentieth century and show us how well God can preserve His Word over time.

The scrolls survived over two thousand years and the original scribes' time capsules help humankind to confirm God's precision and the preservation of His Word.

The Dead Sea Scrolls include well-preserved copies of each Old Testament book except for *Esther*. The miraculously preserved time capsule manuscripts help us answer, "How much do biblical books change as scribes copy other copies of texts for nearly two thousand years?"

Despite rampant cultural skepticism about the Bible and the fidelity of its contents, the Dead Sea Scrolls form the backbone of a powerful experiment that can either help establish, or refute, the reliability of today's assemblage of ancient books we call The Bible.

Figure 5.1 helps us visualize an experiment that scientifically measures changes in Old Testament writings. Envision the Dead Sea Scrolls rolled up, sealed in jars, and placed in deserted caves as we start a stopwatch at 70 A.D. (the latest date scholars assess the burial of the scrolls).[49] Next, we allow our timer to run a minimum of 1877 years. During those 1877 years, many generations of scribes record copies, of copies, of copies of the manuscripts.

Next, we click off our stopwatch during the year (1947 A.D.) when the Scrolls were discovered. Finally, we compare the ancient Dead Sea manuscripts with modern ones. How much did the manuscripts change?

After nearly two thousand years of copying and re-copying the scrolls, the ancient scrolls differed from modern copies by less than 5%. Those differences amounted to typos or misspelled words.

How do we determine, "less than 5%" difference? We can compare, for example, the 166 Hebrew words in Isaiah 53 with the same passage in a modern copy of Isaiah 53. The ancient and modern manuscripts differ by less than 5%. Most of those differences amounted to minor, easily recognizable and correctable typos.

---

[49] Several techniques—including Carbon-14 dating—date the Dead Sea Scrolls between 250 BC to 70 AD. Jeffrey L. Rubenstein, professor of Talmud and Rabbinics at New York University, dated the scrolls from about 200 BC to 70 A.D. We use the latest date in our "experiment."

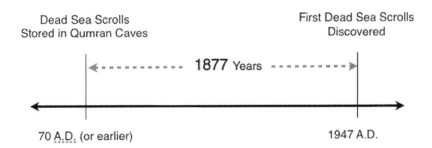

Dead Sea Scrolls
Stored in Qumran Caves

First Dead Sea Scrolls
Discovered

◀ ‑ ‑ ‑ ‑ ‑ ‑ ‑ ‑ ‑ ‑ **1877** Years ‑ ‑ ‑ ‑ ‑ ‑ ‑ ‑ ‑ ‑ ▶

70 A.D. (or earlier)   1947 A.D.

The few differences that separate the Dead Sea Scrolls from later manuscripts prove how well the ancient scribes reproduced the scrolls over two thousand years.

New Testament writings are even more accurate than the Old Testament. More copies in more languages enable highly accurate translations.

Scribes recorded the New Testament books into over 5,000 surviving Greek manuscripts. When we include the Syriac, Latin, and Coptic language translations of the New Testament, that total number of surviving copies grows to over 24,600.[50]

A General Introduction to the Bible states,

> *The New Testament then, has not only survived in more manuscripts than any other book from antiquity, but it has survived in a purer form than any other great book—a form that is 99.5 percent pure.*[51]

Imagine a truth explosion during Jesus' death and resurrection where the "printing presses" ran for many years in many languages. Despite the decay, disintegration, or aging of

[50] Richard M. Fales, Ph.D., *Archaeology and History Attest to the Reliability of the Bible*,

[51] Norman L. Geisler and William E. Nix, A General Introduction to the Bible, (1968; reprint: Chicago, Moody Press, 1980), p. 367.

the original documents, thousands of other manuscripts help scholars resolve any uncertainties.

Our simple Dead Sea Scroll experiment shows no one altered the biblical books beyond a few typos. Plus, mountains of archaeological, scientific, and historical evidence validate the Scroll accounts. The scribes transmitted the Bible we have today in an extremely pure form.

Although the scribes transmitted highly accurate renderings of ancient manuscripts, how do we know God inspired our biblical writings and not the scribes?

Figure 5.1. The Dead Sea Scrolls were hidden in caves near Qumran for a minimum of 1877 years. During this time, Hebrew manuscripts were copied and recopied. When we compare the Qumran manuscripts with todays Hebrew "copies of copies of copies," we discover they differ by a few typos.

A Book that Predicts the Future

Imagine a best friend who accurately predicts events in your life each week for several years—without error. As your friend's predictions each came true, wouldn't you believe his remaining forecasts? Wouldn't you listen to other advice he gave you?

God is such a friend who predicted individual, national, and international events. He gave us His Word through highly detailed and carefully calibrated prophecy. Other religions claim prophecy in their writings, but their few cited examples are nebulous, vague, or self-fulfilling writings that don't qualify as prophetic writings.

The Bible claims it comes from God, not from man and proves its case through numerous, detailed, and precise prophecies. Approximately 30% of the Bible contains prophetic verses[52] and the God of the Bible assures us prophecy never

---

[52] J. Barton Payne, *Encyclopedia of Biblical Prophecy: The Complete Guide to Scriptural Predictions and Their Fulfillment* (Grand Rapids, Mich.: Baker, 1973), 13, 674–675.

came by the will of man, but holy men of God spoke as they were moved by the Holy Spirit.[53]

The following passage reminds us God reveals events in advance:

I am the Lord, that is My name;
And My glory I will not give to another,
Nor My praise to carved images.
Behold, the former things have come to pass,
And new things I declare;
Before they spring forth I tell you of them.[54]

God sets Himself and His writings apart from any other spiritual or religious writings by forecasting the future. His Bible prophecies exceed any other spiritual writings in detail, quality, and quantity.

The God of the Bible incentivized Israel's prophets for reporting only what He gave them; if they were wrong, they could die.

But the prophet who presumes to speak a word in My name, which I have not commanded him to speak, or who speaks in the name of other gods, that prophet shall die.' And if you say in your heart, 'How shall we know the word which the LORD has not spoken?'—when a prophet speaks in the name of the LORD, if the thing does not happen or come to pass, that is the thing which the LORD has not spoken; the prophet has spoken it presumptuously; you shall not be afraid of him![55]

---

[53] 2 Peter 1:21

[54] Isaiah 42:8-9

[55] Deuteronomy 18:20-22

In contrast to the Bible's prophets, the authors of non-biblical religious writings did not risk predicting the future. Since non-biblical scribes could not accurately predict the future without God's inspiration, they simply avoided predictions. Yet, accurately predicting the future is a credential that establishes the Bible's credibility beyond any other religious writings.

Many of God's prophecies focused on Israel and predicted Israel's rise, fall, and restoration. Ezekiel predicted how Israel's enemies would conquer and scatter them to many other countries.

I shall scatter them among the nations, and disperse them in the countries (Ezekiel 12:15).

And I will scatter thee among the heathen, and disperse thee in the countries... (see Ezekiel 22:15; 36:19).

Some biblical prophecies spell out specific consequences. For example, King Solomon quickly broke God's covenant by worshiping other gods. God warned Solomon and Israel that He would remove them from their land if they turned from His commandments:

But if you or your sons at all turn from following Me, and do not keep My commandments and My statutes which I have set before you, but go and serve other gods and worship them, then I will cut off Israel from the land which I have given them; and this house which I have consecrated for My name I will cast out of My sight.[56]

Although Ezekiel predicted Israel's idolatry would lead to their captivity and a desolate land, did that really happen?

Mark Twain describes Israel's landscape during his visit there in the early 1900s.

---

[56] 1 Kings 9:6-7

A desolate country whose soil is rich enough, but is given over wholly to weeds... a silent mournful expanse....a desolation....we never saw a human being on the whole route....hardly a tree or shrub anywhere. Even the olive tree and the cactus, those fast friends of a worthless soil, had almost deserted the country.[57]

Although the Jews had been conquered, banished from their land, and dispersed to the ends of the earth, God restored Israel to her land after two thousand years of desolation, in 1948, just as Ezekiel, Amos, and Jeremiah predicted.

God knew Israel would be banished from their land, but He also knew they would be restored and He had His prophets write about it:

Ezekiel 39:27-29 'When I have brought them back from the nations and have gathered them from the countries of their enemies, I will show myself holy through them in the sight of many nations. Then they will know that I am the LORD their God, for though I sent them into exile among the nations, I will gather them to their own land, not leaving any behind. I will no longer hide my face from them, for I will pour out my Spirit on the house of Israel,' declares the Sovereign LORD.

Amos 9:13-15 'The days are coming,' declares the LORD, 'when the reaper will be overtaken by the plowman and the planter by the one treading grapes. New wine will drip from the mountains and flow from all the hills. I will bring back my exiled people Israel; they will rebuild the ruined cities and live in them. They will plant vineyards and drink their wine; they will make gardens and eat their fruit. I will plant Israel in their own land, never again to be uprooted from the land I have given them,' says the LORD your God.

---

[57] Mark Twain, *The Innocents Abroad,* 1869 Public Domain Edition, p. 267

Jeremiah 30:2 This is what the LORD, the God of Israel, says: Write in a book all the words I have spoken to you. The days are coming, declares the LORD, when I will bring my people Israel and Judah back from captivity and restore them to the land I gave their forefathers to possess,' says the LORD.

Jeremiah 31:10 Hear the word of the LORD, O nations; proclaim it in distant coastlands: 'He who scattered Israel will gather them and will watch over his flock like a shepherd.'

Jeremiah 33:7 I will bring Judah and Israel back from captivity and will rebuild them as they were before.

Ezekiel 37:21-22 I will take the Israelites out of the nations where they have gone. I will gather them from all around and bring them back into their own land. I will make them one nation in the land, on the mountains of Israel. There will be one king over all of them and they will never again be two nations or be divided into two kingdoms.

False prophets of Old Testament times risked severe consequences if they were wrong. God told Israel to kill false prophets that made predictions that did not come to pass.[58] Similarly, the Book of Revelation warns that those who eliminate certain passages or add non-biblical writings to His word will be severely judged.

For I testify to everyone who hears the words of the prophecy of this book: If anyone adds to these things, God will add to him the plagues that are written in this book; and if anyone takes away from the words of the

---

[58] Deuteronomy 13:1-5

book of this prophecy, God shall take away his part from the Book of Life, from the holy city, and from the things which are written in this book.[59]

If you doubt the Bible is superior to any other spiritual writings, simply compare Bible prophecy with the alleged prophecies of any other religious writings.

You could begin your test by compiling a list of all the Bible prophecy. J. Barton Payne's *Encyclopedia of Biblical Prophecy* documents 1,239 prophecies in the Old Testament and 578 prophecies in the New Testament.[60] Another excellent resource is Dr. Walvoord's book, *Every Prophecy of the Bible: Clear Explanations for Uncertain Times.*[61]

Once you have a grasp of the breadth, depth, and detail of the Bible's prophecies, look up the reported prophecies of any other religion on the internet and evaluate how many prophecies those writings report. How detailed are their prophecies? How far in advance of actual events did other religions' prophecies make their predictions? I prefer to let you reach your own conclusions but when I did this exercise, the prophecies of other spiritual writings numbered only four or five. Furthermore, those few prophecies were either vague or self-fulfilling.

The Bible possesses several other credentials that provide additional credibility.

Archeological Evidence

Some experts have tried to disprove the Bible but archaeology affirms the Bible's accounts.

The famous historian and archeologist Sir William Ramsay traveled to Asia Minor to refute the Bible's historicity and

[59] Revelation 22:18-179

[60] J. Barton Payne, *Encyclopedia of Biblical Prophecy: The Complete Guide to Scriptural Predictions and Their Fulfillment (Paperback),* by Baker Books, 1996

[61] John F. Walvoord, *Every Prophecy of the Bible: Clear Explanations for Uncertain Times* (Paperback)
by David C. Cook, 2011

accuracy. He focused his skepticism on Luke's detailed accounts in the Gospel of Luke and the Book of Acts.

In dig after dig, Ramsay discovered detailed evidence that supported Luke's accounts. Ramsay's archaeological team excavated, and found Governors mentioned by Luke that many historians never believed existed. Without a single error, Luke accurately named thirty-two countries, fifty-four cities, and nine islands.

Ramsay notes, *Luke is a historian of the first rank; not merely are his statements of fact trustworthy . . . this author should be placed along with the very greatest historians.*[62]

Although he intended to disprove and discredit Luke's accounts, Ramsay became so overwhelmed with the archaeological evidence corroborating Luke's writings, he became Christian.

I began with a mind unfavorable to it . . . but more recently I found myself brought into contact with the Book of Acts as an authority for the topography, antiquities, and society of Asia Minor. It was gradually borne upon me that in various details the narrative showed marvelous truth.[63]

The classical historian A.N. Sherwin-White observes, *any attempt to reject its basic historicity even in matters of detail must now appear absurd. Roman historians have long taken biblical accuracy for granted.*[64]

The Jewish archeologist Nelson Glueck sums up the Bible's archaeological credentials.

It may be stated categorically that no archeological discovery has ever controverted a single biblical

[62] A. N. Sherwin-White, *Roman Society and Roman Law in the New Testament*, Clarendon Press, 1963, pg. 189

[63] Ramsay, William M. *St. Paul the Traveler and the Roman Citizen*, Baker,1982 p. 8

[64] Josh McDowell, *The New Evidence That Demands a Verdict*, Thomas Nelson Publishers, 1999 p. 64

reference. Scores of archeological findings have been made which confirm in clear outline or in exact detail historical statements in the Bible.[65]

Glueck next cites archaeological evidence as Babylon, Medo-Persia, Greece, and the Roman empires rose to power and then fell, as recorded in the Book of Daniel's second chapter. Archaeology also supports findings related to the tower of Babel, events in Exodus, the walls of Jericho, and the tombs of St. Paul's contemporaries.

Whereas archeology supports biblical accounts, other spiritual writings lack evidence for even the simplest archeological artifacts. Nelson Glueck faults the Book of Mormon's lack of archeological support.

Even the most common of items in their scripture's pages have never be found. This includes swords (3 Nephi 1:18), scimitars (Alma 2:12), chariots (Alma 18:12), large buildings (Ether 10:5), many highways (Helaman 14:24), forts (Alma 48:8), javelins (Alma 51:34), breastplates (Mosiah 8:10), hand plates (Alma 46:13), compasses (Alma 37:38,44), trumpets (3 Nephi 13:2), chains (2 Nephi 1:13), hoes (Ether 10:25), and harps (2 Nephi 15:12).

While not everything in the Bible has been discovered—there's still a lot of work to do—only speculation takes place in Mormon circles. This is why Mormon scholars cannot agree on where the Book of Mormon lands really are. Non-biblical writings often describe people, places, and objects that archaeology shows to be false.[66]

---

[65] Glueck, Nelson, *Rivers in the Desert*, New York: Grove Press, 1959, pp. 31-32.

[66] *Archeology and the Book of Mormon,* Mormonism Research Ministry, accessed on August 14, 2014, http://www.mrm.org/bofm-archaeology,

Archeologists never found the cities or the simplest artifacts described in the *Book of Mormon*. There should be hundreds of thousands of artifacts discovered by now if the *Book of Mormon* were true. How can we trust the *Book of Mormon* if archaeologists and other historical documents cannot identify the people, places, and things it describes?

In contrast to the lack of archeological evidence for the Book of Mormon, Yale University archeologist Millar Burrows observed,

Archeological work has unquestionably strengthened confidence in the reliability of the scriptural record. More than one archeologist has found respect for the Bible increased by the experience of excavation in Palestine. [67]

The Bible's critics are routinely embarrassed by discoveries that corroborate Bible accounts they previously declared myth.

For example, the Bible described the Hittites, King David, Caiaphas, and Pontius Pilate before anyone discovered archaeological evidence about them. The skeptics naturally declared the Biblical accounts of these people as inaccurate— and by implication, they questioned the accuracy of the rest of the Bible. Archaeologists uncovered artifacts that clearly certified the existence of the Hittites, David, Caiaphas, Pilate. and many other biblical people.[68]

Skeptics frequently forget the Bible provides a first-rate historical record. The Bible often surpasses secular records as it documents and details historical events.

The biblical scholar R.D.Wilson—fluent in several ancient languages and dialects—meticulously analyzed twenty-nine kings from ten different nations. Each king was corroborated by archeological artifacts. Wilson then compared secular sources with the biblical accounts. His findings?

---

[67] Millar Burrows, *What Mean These Stones? (New York: Meridian Books, 1956), p.1*

[68] *The Trustworthiness of the Bible,* Calvary Chapel, accessed July 1, 2015, http://calvarychapel.com/series/is-god-dead/view/the-trustworthiness-of-the-bible/

Wilson showed that the names as recorded in the Bible not only matched the artifacts perfectly, but accurately lists the chronology of the kings. To the contrary, Wilson showed that the Librarian of Alexandria, Ptolemy, and Herodotus recorded many names incorrectly. Secular sources frequently misspelled names, or their recorded names did not match artifacts or monuments.[69]

Rampant archeological evidence found in Israel and the Mideast compel many honest skeptics to acknowledge the historical veracity of the Bible and many have even surrendered their lives to Jesus.

Unlike other spiritual writings, the Bible uniquely exhibits stable texts, prophecy, history, and archeology. It also exhibits a range of scientific information that science would not "discover" for several thousand years.

Is the Bible Scientific?

Despite the historical, archeological, and prophetic evidence that underpin historical accounts, few today regard the Bible as a "scientific" book. Although the Bible is primarily a historical and spiritual set of writings, it includes scientific knowledge that couldn't be proven for hundreds or thousands of years. In contrast, other spiritual writings either contain no scientific facts, or they get them wrong.

Philosophy poured foundations for dismantling truth in the late 1800s in Europe. The West inherited and incubated these philosophies in the early 1900s. The 1950s and 60s ushered in modernism that tried to separate spiritual truths from physical ones. Modernism elevated science above spiritual truth claims and seemed to say, since we cannot physically measure or sense God, He is not real—or at least not as authentic as "scientific" truths.[70]

---

[69] *Archaeological Evidence*, BibleEvidences.com, accessed 1 July 2015, http://www.bibleevidences.com/archeology.htm

[70] Francis A. Schaeffer, *How Should We Then Live?*, Crossway Books, Wheaton, IL, pp. 144-166

Modernism matured and morphed throughout the 1970s and 80s into postmodernism. Key parts of postmodern philosophy rigged a "Does truth exist at all?" question so it could deliver its grim, pre-postured answer—truth is dead and so is God.

However, few postmodernists live as if truth is dead. The most devout postmodernist knows it's absolutely true that if he jumps from the top of a cliff, the invisible force of gravity will kill him; he knows his beliefs or disbeliefs will not change gravity's deadly consequences.

Science develops methods and tools that enhance how we understand the universe. Telescopes probe the universe as microscopes help us peer into cells.

Science delivers technology for aircraft, cars, computers, televisions, microwave ovens, cell phones, etc.

Scientists apply methods to understand God's creation. They observe, hypothesize, experiment, and adjust their theories until they align with reality.

Biblical prophets present scientific knowledge that came from God. They report knowledge that must have sounded irrational to the scientists of their day.

A spherical earth suspended on nothing clashed with human intuition and science of our ancient world. However, Isaiah 40:22 describes a "circle" world that Job 26:7 claims hangs on nothing!

Non-biblical spiritual writings either contain no foreknowledge, or else modern science has overturned their faulty reporting. For example, some ancients believed in a flat earth resting on the backs of animals.

Many from antiquity also believed the earth had always existed but modern   science says no.

Another question that comes to mind is whether or not space and time existed prior to the big bang. A trio of highly respected astrophysicists have published papers plainly saying no. Steven Hawking, George Ellis, and Roger Penrose based their work on the basics of Einstein's theory of general relativity. Their calculations led them to believe that time and space had a definite beginning and the beginning corresponds directly with the big bang. In other words, the big bang was the beginning of everything.[71]

The Bible teaches us that God created *the heaven and the earth* (Genesis 1:1). The big-bang theory agrees with some of the biblical description, but prefers not to acknowledge God's role and therefore has one serious, logical flaw.

If something can's come from nothing, where did all the matter and energy *come from that went "bang"?* It came from our Creator.

According to the Bible, the world will also end.

But the day of the Lord will come as a thief in the night, in which the heavens will pass away with a great noise, and the elements will melt with fervent heat; both the earth and the works that are in it will be burned up. Therefore, since all these things will be dissolved, what manner of persons ought you to be in holy conduct and godliness.[72]

Hebrews 1:10-12 and much of Revelation describes the inevitable end of our world and universe before God restores everything.

Science in Job's and Jonah's days could not have guessed "springs" are pouring water from the bottom of the sea (Job 38:16). Nor could they have seen "mountains" on the bottom of our oceans (Jonah 2:5-6). Submarines can now confirm the foreknowledge Job's and Jonah's predictions.

Solomon describes the earth's general hydrological cycle; *all the rivers flow into the sea, yet the sea is not full. To the place where the rivers flow, there they flow again* (Ecclesiastes 1:7). Thousands of years before scientists understood invisible water vapor, Job provides detail to Solomon's assessment.

For He draws up drops of water,

---

[71] *What is the Big Bang Theory?* The Universe Today, accessed 3 July 2015, http://www.universetoday.com/54756/what-is-the-big-bang-theory

[72] 2 Peter 3:10-11

Which distill as rain from the mist,
Which the clouds drop down
And pour abundantly on man.
Indeed, can anyone understand the spreading of clouds,
The thunder from His canopy? [73]

In addition to scientific foreknowledge, the Bible's credibility is aided by detailed archaeological discoveries. The Bible's critics are routinely embarrassed by previously undiscovered artifacts that corroborate Bible accounts. Such discoveries resolve truth claims the biblical skeptics declared myth.

For example, the Bible described the Hittites, King David, and Pontius Pilate before anyone discovered archaeological evidence about them. The skeptics naturally declared the Biblical accounts of these people as inaccurate—and by implication, they questioned the accuracy of the rest of the Bible. Archaeologists soon uncovered artifacts that clearly certified the existence of the Hittites, David, and Pilate.

Skeptics frequently forget the Bible provides a first-rate historical record and often surpasses secular records as it documents and details factual events.

The biblical scholar R.D. Wilson—fluent in several ancient languages and dialects—meticulously analyzed twenty-nine kings from ten different nations. Each king was corroborated by archeological artifacts. Wilson

Most who criticize the Bible for alleged contradictions cannot name one. Many who claim the Bible contradicted itself have never investigated alleged inconsistencies, and others cannot name one contradiction in the Bible.

Many others assume that differences in statements equate to contradiction when they do not.

For example, if Proverbs 26:4 teaches us not to answer a fool according to his folly and Proverbs 26:5 tells us to answer a fool in his folly. Why isn't this contradiction?

The Bible often reflects wise situational awareness and prescribes various responses to different types of people.

---

[73] Job 36:27-29

Sometimes it's best to answer foolish people in their tone; other times not.

Others claim the Bible contradicts itself because genealogies differ. How can we possibly reconcile the different genealogies recorded in Matthew 1 and Luke 3? Matt Slick sheds some light.

Notice that Luke starts with Mary and goes backwards to Adam. Matthew starts with Abraham and goes forward to Joseph. The intents of the genealogies were obviously different which is clearly seen in their styles. Luke was not written to the Jews but Matthew was. Therefore, Matthew would carry the legal line (from Abraham through David) and Luke the biological one (from Adam through David). Also, notice that Luke's first three chapters mention Mary eleven times, hence, the genealogy from her. Fourth, notice Luke 3:23, "And when He began His ministry, Jesus Himself was about thirty years of age, being supposedly the son of Joseph, the son of Eli." This designation "supposedly" seems to signify the Marian genealogy since it seems to indicate that Jesus is not the biological son of Joseph. [74]

Some presume that since the Bible's books record different durations for the reigns of certain kings, that it contradicts itself, but it does not. These differences make sense when we consider that the Bible's books were written by different prophets from different regions, with different customs, and different ways standards they used for recording their events and chronologies.

For example, some biblical writers counted partial years of a king's reign as full years, and others counted only complete years. Once we understand the differences in these standards, we find consistency instead of discrepancy. Many of those who have tried to challenge the Bible's reliability have been convinced of the opposite as they conducted their own research.

---

[74] Matt Slick, *Why are there different genealogies for Jesus in Matthew 1 and Luke 3?* www.carm.org [accessed 20 September 2014]

Lee Strobel, for example, attempted to disprove the Bible's reliability as he applied his legal, and investigative journalism skills. He located and interviewed world-renowned experts in various fields and challenged them in many areas. Lee surrendered his life to Christ after discovering how true, detailed, and reliable the Bible's accounts actually were.

Although it is beyond the scope of this book to address in detail other criticisms levied against the Bible, Lee Strobel's book, *The Case for Christ,* explores and resolves a full range of biblical criticisms in an easy to understand style.[75] Lee followed the pattern of many who tried to disprove the Bible. As he researched the issues that separated him from the Bible and Christ, Lee found overwhelming evidence that Jesus is who He said He was, and God was able to deliver and protect His message in the Bible.

New Testament Credentials

Jesus' birthday is more easily accepted, for most, than the fact He rose from the dead. Yet, without His resurrection, Christianity would be pointless. The Apostle Paul clarifies a powerful reason for Jesus' resurrection:

He has appointed a day on which He will judge the world in righteousness by the Man whom He has ordained. He has given assurance of this to all by raising Him from the dead.[76]

Critics of Jesus' resurrection accounts in Matthew, Mark, Luke, and John often fail to realize the New Testament was written, transcribed, translated, and distributed while hundreds of eyewitnesses were still living.

Living eyewitnesses could easily expose fraud in the New Testament accounts in their day, if any existed, and Christianity would have quickly fizzled out.

---

[75] Lee Strobel, *The Case for Christ*, Zondervan Publishing (1998)

[76] Acts 17:31

62

Similarly, some today unsuccessfully deny Hitler's horrendous murder of millions of innocent Jews during World War II. Not only are Jews alive who experienced the Holocaust, but there are still remnants and artifacts of the death camps remain along with photographs, videos, and surviving guards who worked at the camps and substantiate the atrocity.

Likewise, to convince anyone Jesus did not rise from the dead with so much evidence and so many living eyewitnesses is difficult.

However, the gospels record eyewitness biographical accounts of Jesus' supernatural life, death, and resurrection. These accounts were often punctuated with powerful signs, wonders, and miracles.

> *And Jesus cried out again with a loud voice, and yielded up His spirit. And behold, the veil of the temple was torn in two from top to bottom; and the earth shook and the rocks were split. The tombs were opened, and many bodies of the saints who had fallen asleep were raised; and coming out of the tombs after His resurrection they entered the holy city and appeared to many. Now the centurion, and those who were with him keeping guard over Jesus, when they saw the earthquake and the things that were happening, became very frightened and said, "Truly this was the Son of God!"[77]*

Imagine watching the sky darken, as rocks split and people leave their graves! Then, three days later, Jesus vacates *His* tomb and appears to many individuals and over five hundred witnesses at one time.

Supernatural events calibrated Jesus' messages. The explosion of miracles confronted Jesus' enemies and first-century spin doctors. Certainly the centurion at the foot of the cross understood they had crucified the Son of God.

---

[77] Matthew 27: 50-54

Making matters worse for the skeptics, the apostles followed Jesus' example and, after they were empowered by the Holy Spirit, they continued the signs, wonders, and miracles Jesus performed—including raising people from the dead.

> *And in a window sat a certain young man named Eutychus, who was sinking into a deep sleep. He was overcome by sleep; and as Paul continued speaking, he fell down from the third story and was taken up dead. But Paul went down, fell on him, and embracing him said, 'Do not trouble yourselves, for his life is in him.' Now when he had come up, had broken bread and eaten, and talked a long while, even till daybreak, he departed. And they brought the young man in alive, and they were not a little comforted.* [78]

Despite those who dilute, diminish, or deny Jesus' miracles, Jesus' enemies purport the Roman guards fell asleep. Then, they asserted that the apostles allegedly stole Jesus' body from the tomb. Throughout their fictitious stories, they acknowledged a pivotal truth: Jesus' tomb was empty.

Their cover up story contained many gaping holes. For example, why would the apostles, too afraid to stand by Jesus at His crucifixion (except for John), risk their lives to rescue Jesus' dead body?

From the apostles' perspective, *why should I risk my life to start a new religion based upon a lie?* Even if someone wanted to steal Jesus' body and perpetuate a resurrection story, a contingent of Roman guards and a huge rock covering the tomb made stealing Jesus' body impossible that night.

The mouth of the tomb, for example, was sealed with a large wheel-shaped stone weighing up to 2 tons. One theory supposes the apostles could have moved such a stone as the soldiers guarding Jesus' tomb slept peacefully. Under Roman law, sleeping soldiers risked death for dereliction of duty.

---

[78] Acts 20:9-12

Those who ran, hid, or denied Jesus at His arrest and crucifixion would now die as willing martyrs rather than deny Jesus. Something changed; they could no longer deny or renounce Jesus as Lord. Were they deceived?

No, the disciples now knew the truth; Jesus arose from the dead as He predicted and promised. Hundreds saw Him and many disciples spoke with Jesus, touched Him, and saw Him eat.

The Apostle John explains his experience and his motivation for recording these events:

That which was from the beginning, which we have heard, which we have seen with our eyes, which we have looked upon, and our hands have handled, concerning the Word of life—the life was manifested, and we have seen, and bear witness, and declare to you that eternal life which was with the Father and was manifested to us—that which we have seen and heard we declare to you, that you also may have fellowship with us; and truly our fellowship is with the Father and with His Son Jesus Christ. And these things we write to you that your joy may be full.[79]

Miracles continued with Jesus' resurrection. Jesus' faithful followers brought divine healing and raised people from the dead Just as their master had done. After Jesus rose from the dead and ascended into Heaven, he appeared to one of the most notorious persecutors of Christians and converted him into the most notable apostle, evangelist, and miracle-worker in the New Testament record.

Now Saul, still breathing threats and murder against the disciples of the Lord, went to the high priest, and asked for letters from him to the synagogues at Damascus, so that if he found any belonging to the Way, both men and women, he might bring them bound to

---

[79] 1 John 1:1-4

Jerusalem. As he was traveling, it happened that he was approaching Damascus, and suddenly a light from heaven flashed around him; and he fell to the ground and heard a voice saying to him, 'Saul, Saul, why are you persecuting Me?' And he said, 'Who are You, Lord?' And He said, 'I am Jesus whom you are persecuting, but get up and enter the city, and it will be told you what you must do. [80]

Besides converted lives, other signs, wonders, and miracles followed Jesus and His disciples. Many discount those signs merely because the Bible records them. However, Jesus' miracles were also documented in other first-century sources.

Roman historian Velleius describes how Jesus of Nazareth brought a dead baby back to life.

According to Velleius, that great man's name was Iēsous de Nazarenus, a Greco-Latin translation of Jesus' Hebrew name, Yeshua haNotzri.

Upon entering town, Jesus would have visited the house of a woman named Elisheba, who had just given birth to a stillborn child. Jesus picked up the dead child and uttered a prayer in Aramaic to the heavens, which unfortunately the author describes as "immensus," meaning incomprehensible. To the crowd's surprise and amazement, the baby came back to life almost immediately, crying and squirming like a healthy newborn. [81]

Jesus' miracles fulfill prophecy and authenticate His salvation message. We can almost hear Jesus say, "I sacrificed myself to pay for your sins. I do not want to be apart from you for eternity,

---

[80] Acts 9:1-6, NASB

[81] Newly-Found Document Holds Eyewitness Account of Jesus Performing Miracle, http://worldnewsdailyreport.com/newly-found-document-holds-eyewitness-account-of-jesus-performing-miracle/#sthash.pMAaw4N2.dpuf. [viewed 10 October 2014]

will you receive me? I do not care about church attendance. I care about your surrendered heart in relationship and fellowship with Me."

If the Bible conveys an accurate portrait of Jesus and His love for us, and we've never read or studied the Bible for ourselves, how would we know if we distorted HIs character? Could we have missed what He really wants from us?

Chapter 6
Caricatures of Christ

Beware lest anyone cheat you through philosophy and empty deceit, according to the tradition of men, according to the basic principles of the world, and not according to Christ. (Colossians 2:8)

Ivan Pavlov won his Nobel Prize in 1904 for contributing to medicine and physiology.[82] Although Ivan's research focused on animal digestion, He also impacted the field of psychology and uncovered important linkages related to animal and human conditioning. Conditioning?

If you've had pets, you may have conditioned them. Each time goldfish see your hand approaching their bowl with food, they become "conditioned" as they begin associating your hand with dinner time. They anxiously circle the bowl or snap their mouths at the water's surface as they anticipate your hand delivering their meal.

Eventually, the goldfish respond to a hand as if they will be fed—even if the hand contains no food. Likewise, cats and dogs may lick their lips when they hear you open a can of cat food or rustle their food bag.

Pavlov also noticed these effects and as he collected dog saliva for digestion research, he noticed his lab dogs drooled before they were fed. He also observed, over time, that his dogs salivated when they saw the white lab coats of the researchers who fed them. Ivan now wondered if he could substitute another stimulus for the lab coats.

He tested his theory and rang a bell before feeding the dogs. As Pavlov expected, the dogs eventually salivated to the sound of

---

[82] Nobelprize.org, *Ivan Pavlov - Biographical*, accessed on 11 July 2015, http://www.nobelprize.org/nobel_prizes/medicine/laureates/1904/pavlov-bio.html

the bell alone. The ringing bell built anticipation into the dogs who knew after the bell sounded, they would soon receive food. They became conditioned to the bell.

Pavlov further discovered that the conditioning of his dogs faded over time. If food didn't accompany the bell, the dogs eventually ignored the bell and "disassociated" it from their food.

In another example, if you've taped the side of an aquarium, the fish flinch. If you keep tap again, the fish "jitter" less and less. Eventually, the fish will not react to the tapping.

People also stop responding to certain stimuli. For example, as a car alarm sounds in a parking lot, many assume the alarm malfunctioned and do not call the police.

We can easily test for religious conditioning and desensitization as we examine some common caricatures of Christ we may have built in our minds. Are you ready to test your beliefs for caricatures of Christ?

What is the first thing that comes into your mind as you read, "Jesus?"

Really answer that question—what came to your mind?

Did you think religion, church, church people?

When artists create caricatures, they exaggerate some features of their subjects and minimize others. Caricature artists create recognizable, distorted, and often humorous renderings of their subjects.

Similarly, spiritual deception creates caricatures of Christ in our minds by exaggerating some of His features and minimizing others. These caricatures form nearly indelible impressions of God that oppose the character of the God of the Bible. The Bible is a powerful tool for dismantling caricatures of God, so we can identify the True God.

I never followed the Apostle Paul's advice (to compare my beliefs about the Bible, with the Bible itself)[83] until I was in my late

---

[83] Acts 17:11

thirties. As I studied the Bible, I was astonished how much my impressions of the Bible differed from the Bible's actual teachings.

Many rightly presume their religion was built upon a solid foundation of Scripture. However, strong Scriptural foundations, stressed by human agendas, can crack and become overgrown with ritual, traditions, religious doctrines, and false teachings. Few test their religions for foundation problems, and neglect studying Scripture for themselves.

Do you feel comfortable with your spiritual or religious beliefs? Spiritual deception almost always makes us feel comfortable too. Comfort doesn't make beliefs true, only when we align our beliefs with the truth can we say we have true beliefs.

How closely does the Jesus of your beliefs match the Jesus of Scripture?

As we expose some caricatures of Christ, see if you recognize any of them in your church or yourself.

Hypocritical Caricature of Christ

Some develop a caricature of Christ that equates Jesus with hypocritical church people. Hypocrites cause us to bundle the True Jesus so tightly with religion, that when religious people or religious systems fail, Jesus seems to fail.

Often, victims of hypocrisy abandon the Jesus of the Bible because they were victimized by a religious human who did not represent the Biblical Christ.

The Jesus of the Bible detests hypocrisy, condemns hypocrites, and pronounces three "woes" on them.

But woe to you, scribes and Pharisees, hypocrites! For you shut up the kingdom of heaven against men; for you neither go in yourselves, nor do you allow those who are entering to go in. Woe to you, scribes and Pharisees, hypocrites! For you devour widows' houses, and for a pretense make long prayers. Therefore you will receive greater condemnation. Woe to you, scribes and Pharisees, hypocrites! For you travel land and sea

to win one proselyte, and when he is won, you make him
twice as much a son of hell as yourselves.[84]

If you've been alienated from God by a wolf in sheep's clothing, it pays to ask, *did a religious person offend me, or did Jesus offend me?*

Good Works Caricature of Christ

Can you imagine a Christian church that would lock Jesus out? Some lock Him out of their hearts as they unknowingly substitute their "good works" for the salvation Jesus bought for them with His blood.

Churches cool down when they falsely rely on their good deeds and churches to save them instead of receiving their Savior.

Once we allow Jesus access to our hearts, we will passionately pursue *His* good works and not our own.

The spiritual temperature of entire churches can cool to lukewarm if they misunderstand what the Bible teaches about works.

Is your church (or heart) on fire for God, or has it cooled off?

I know your works, that you are neither cold nor hot. I
could wish you were cold or hot. So then, because you
are lukewarm, and neither cold nor hot, I will vomit you
out of My mouth. Because you say, 'I am rich, have
become wealthy, and have need of nothing'—and do not
know that you are wretched, miserable, poor, blind, and
naked.[85]

Many churches teach we attain Heaven by following their doctrines and doing good deeds. However, breaking one commandment one time breaks God's entire law (James 2:10).

---

[84] Matthew 23:13-15

[85] Revelation 3:15-17

What if we truly believed our salvation comes by grace alone, through faith alone,[86] in Christ alone?[87] Suppose Jesus finished everything necessary for Heaven and our only "work" is to receive Him with our hearts?

Doesn't God want us to do good deeds?

He does, if we allow Him to direct us toward the works He ordained for us from before the foundation of the world (Ephesians 2:10). Our good works should flow as a byproduct of our relationship with Jesus but deeds don't cause right relationship with God.[88]

We can unravel the good works caricature by following Jesus' advice to the lukewarm Laodicean church.

Behold, I stand at the door and knock. If anyone hears My voice and opens the door, I will come in to him and dine with him, and he with Me.[89]

Have you truly invited Jesus into your heart and surrendered your life to Him, or do you pursue "good" works in a futile attempt to earn your salvation?

Some avoid committing their lives to Jesus because they believe He might change them—and thankfully, He will!

Soft-on-Sin Caricature of Christ

Jesus allowed Himself to be crucified so that we could escape sin and hell. Out of His love for each of us, Christ paid for our sins with His sacrifice, so we could escape the Lake of Fire. However, many fail to find the relevance of Jesus' gospel in their lives because they don't see they have a sin problem.

Few churches would say they endorse sin, but many redefine it or don't mention it in their services. Soft-on-sin churches often

---

[86] Ephesians 2:8-9

[87] See Romans 10:9

[88] Isaiah 64:6

[89] Revelation 3:20

preach an imbalanced message that focuses us on God's grace, without considering His view of sin.

Soft-on-sin caricatures may teach that since God is love, He refuses to judge, or send anyone to Hell. The "cheap grace" god differs from The God of the Bible who teaches divine judgment and consequences for sin.

Now the works of the flesh are evident, which are: adultery, fornication, uncleanness, lewdness, idolatry, sorcery, hatred, contentions, jealousies, outbursts of wrath, selfish ambitions, dissensions, heresies, envy, murders, drunkenness, revelries, and the like; of which I tell you beforehand, just as I also told you in time past, that those who practice such things will not inherit the kingdom of God.[90]

Two first-century churches not only softened their stances on sin, but promoted it. The churches of Pergamos[91] and Thyatira,[92] either tolerated, or taught sexual immorality.

As modern churches grow soft on sin; they often overemphasize grace, and de-emphasize sin.

When I searched online Bibles for "sin" and "grace," I discovered *sin* occurred almost four hundred times and *grace* appeared less than one hundred and sixty-four times. If the Bible teaches about sin over three times as much as it teaches about grace, maybe more churches should pay attention to what God says about sin. Does yours?

The soft-on-sin caricature makes it difficult to receive Jesus' payment for their sins if they don't understand the *cost* of their sins—or that they even *have* any.

Many modern churches teach or permit sin and ignore God's hatred of sin. Although God's grace alone saves us from sin's penalties, we must first understand sin is the reason Jesus died

---

[90] Galatians 5:19-21

[91] Revelation 2:12-17

[92] Revelation 2:18-29

on the cross to pay our penalty *for* something; that something is sin.

Although the soft-on-sin caricature overemphasizes grace, the legalist caricature overemphasizes the Law and misconstrue's its purpose.

Legalist Caricature of Christ

Legalist and goodness caricatures make us jump through hoops; some jump through good works hoops to earn Heaven while others jump through keep-the-Law hoops to avoid Hell.

The legalist caricature thrives on elevating ritual and human doctrines as means to salvation. It portrays the illusion that we earn Heaven by trying to keep God's Law.

No one but Jesus kept the Law perfectly, and each of us has already broken God's laws many times. Some try to keep the Law as another "good work" that doesn't make us right before the God of the Bible. If the Law doesn't justify us, what does?

Therefore we conclude that a man is justified by faith, without the deeds of the law.[93]

If we are justified[94] solely by faith, why does the Bible teach about the Law so much? The Law shows us how sinful we look to God and points us toward our need for our Savior.

Wherefore the law was our schoolmaster to bring us unto Christ, that we might be justified by faith. But after that faith is come, we are no longer under a schoolmaster.[95]

---

[93] Romans 3:28

[94] Justification means being made right with God. Justification means *just as if I'd never sinned.*

[95] Galatians 3:24-25

74

Many feel they still can earn salvation by keeping most of the Law most of the time. However, as James 2:10 teaches, if we break even one commandment once, we break God's *entire* law.

Legalist caricatures keep us busy doing, doing, doing[96] while Jesus's sacrifice is done, done, done![97] Jesus' sacrifice alone removes our sins.[98] After we receive Christ with our hearts, we'll want to obey Him out of love and as we do, we will automatically develop character through the Holy Spirit that will bring us *beyond* the Law.

Jesus sums up the Law as loving God with our whole heart, and loving our neighbors as ourselves.[99]

We defeat the legalist caricature by understanding the Law's purpose, the motive of our works, and the nature of grace.

For by grace you have been saved through faith, and that not of yourselves; it is the gift of God, not of works, lest anyone should boast. For we are His workmanship, created in Christ Jesus for good works, which God prepared beforehand that we should walk in them.[100]

Our mission, if we have received Christ, is to recognize and "walk out" His good works for us instead of creating our own "good works" resumes.

We shatter this caricature by studying verses about the relationships between the Law, faith, and grace.

Although we've examined common ways church and culture distort Jesus' character, the biggest question separating Jesus from any other religion or philosophy remains: Is Jesus God? That single question separates biblical Christianity from nearly every world religion.

---

[96] Without knowing if we've ever done enough.

[97] See Hebrews 10:10

[98] See Romans 10:9

[99] Matthew 22:37-39

[100] Ephesians 2:8-10

Are you ready to answer the question that may have separated you from God? If so, read on!

CHAPTER 7
Is Jesus God?

The woman said to Him, 'I know that Messiah is coming (who is called Christ).
When He comes, He will tell us all things.'
Jesus said to her, 'I who speak to you am He.' (John 4:25-26)

Dr. Donald Whitaker traveled to a party in California in 1975. After several days, he experienced intense pain and flew back to Oklahoma City where doctors diagnosed him with a fatal disease: acute hemorrhagic necrotic pancreatitis.

Although unable to speak, he heard the medical staff chatter about how sick he was, and how he wouldn't make it out of the hospital alive.

Dr. Whitaker observed, "It's easy to be an atheist when everything is going well, but atheism is much more difficult when you're on your deathbed." You ask yourself things like, "What if they're right and God is real?"

Donald asked the hospital to contact an old friend named Ron and ask him to come to the hospital. Many times in the past, Ron and Dr. Whitaker debated Jesus and His salvation, but now, death and Hell were literally at Whitaker's door.

As hospital staff tried to locate Ron, Donald Whitaker described how he faded away from life a number of times, left his body, and experienced darkness that penetrated his very being. Each time he left his body, terror gripped him because he knew his soul would go to Hell. Whitaker explained, "People talk about warmth and love and light [as they die]. I felt none of that. I felt untold terror."

Donald knew if he slipped all the way into death he would never get back. He desperately struggled to stay alive until he could hear and receive the Gospel from his friend Ron.

As death's bone-chilling cold crept up Donald's legs, Ron finally arrived and announced, "Now is the time."

Ron showed Donald Whitaker where the Bible taught Jesus died for the world's sins. He then led him in a simple prayer to receive Jesus. Donald's terror evaporated, and so did his acute hemorrhagic necrotic pancreatitis. After Donald received Jesus as his Savior, God reversed Dr. Donald Whitaker's fatal disease and changed his life. Donald served the Lord for thirty-two years before passing into Heaven on 10 August 2007.[101]

Jesus claims divinity in the Bible. Jesus' assertion separates Him from any other world religious leader and distinguishes Biblical Christianity from any other religion. No other religious founders claimed to be God, except Jesus. No spiritual leader sacrificed himself to pay for the sins of the world except Jesus.

"Jesus Christ" can mean "Jesus the Messiah," or "Jesus the Anointed One." Let's examine a familiar Christmas story about the Messiah. God's prophets forecasted important details about the coming Messiah so we could recognize Him.

Although you may have heard these details before, can you guess their origin? The Old Testament or the New?

The Messiah will descend from Shem, Abraham, Isaac, Jacob, Judah, Jesse and David. He will be born in the city of Bethlehem in the county of Ephrathah when a bright star appears. It will be a miraculous, virgin birth.

The Messiah will be unique, having preexisted His birth. He will perform many miracles: calming the sea,

---

[101] Atheist Medical Doctor Donald Whittaker has Near death Experience—to Hell and Back. proofthebibleistrue.com, accessed 1 November 2014.

causing the blind to see, the deaf to hear, the lame to walk, and the mute to talk. He will be referred to in many ways, including: God With Us, Wonderful Counselor, Mighty God, Everlasting Father, and Prince of Peace. He will be a great teacher and will use parables.

The Messiah will come to save mankind. He will become man's sin offering and present Himself to Jerusalem as both the anointed King and the Passover Lamb. This will occur 173,880 days after the decree by Artaxerxes to rebuild both Jerusalem and the temple. So, in early April, 33 AD, the Messiah will present Himself to a rejoicing Jerusalem riding on a donkey. But then He will suffer greatly. Many will reject Him, including His friends. He will be betrayed by a friend for 30 pieces of silver. Later, that money will be thrown on the floor of the temple and will eventually go to a potter. At His trial He will not defend Himself. He will say nothing except as required by law. Israel will reject Him.

The Messiah will be taken to a mountaintop identified to Abraham as Moriah, where "the Lord will provide." There He will be crucified with His hands and feet pierced. His enemies will encircle Him, mocking Him, and will cast lots for His clothing. He will call to God, asking why He was "forsaken." He will be given gall and wine. He will die with thieves. But, unlike the thieves, none of His bones will be broken. His heart will fail, as indicated by blood and water spilling out when He is pierced with a spear. He will be buried in a rich man's grave. In three days, He will rise from the dead.[102]

[102] "AllAboutGOD.com Ministries, M. Houdmann, P. Matthews-Rose, R. Niles, editors, 2002-2014. Used by permission.

Although this passage read like a New Testament Christmas story, it was composed entirely from Old Testament prophecy. We prove this by repeating the passage with Old Testament references.

The Messiah preexists time (Gen. 1:1). He is the eternal Redeemer that will come to earth to reconcile mankind with God (Job 19:25-26). Although Satan will try to attack Him, the Messiah will have ultimate victory (Gen. 3:15). One day He will rule over everything and all nations will bow down to Him (Is 45:23, Ps 22).

The Messiah will descend from Shem (Gen 9 –10), Abraham (Gen 22:18), Isaac (Gen 26:4), Jacob (Gen 28:14), Judah (Gen 49:10), Jesse (Is 11:1--5) and David (2 Sam 7:11--16). He will be born in the city of Bethlehem in the county of Ephrathah (Mic 5:2) when a bright star appears (Num 24:17). It will be a miraculous, virgin birth (Is 7:14).

The Messiah will be unique, having preexisted His birth (Mic 5:2). He will perform many miracles: calming the sea (Ps 107:29), causing the blind to see, the deaf to hear, the lame to walk, and the mute to talk (Is 35:4--6). He will be referred to in many ways, including: God With Us (Is 7:14), Wonderful Counselor, Mighty God, Everlasting Father, and Prince of Peace (Is 9:6). He will be a great teacher and will use parables (Ps 78:2).

But the Messiah will come to save mankind (Is 53:3-9). He will become man's sin offering (Is 53:3-9) and present Himself to Jerusalem as both the anointed King (Zech 9:9) and the Passover Lamb (Is 53:3-9). This will occur 173,880 days after the decree by Artaxerxes to rebuild both Jerusalem and the temple (Dan 9:20-27). So, in early April, 33 AD, the Messiah will present Himself to a rejoicing Jerusalem riding on a donkey (Zech 9:9). But then He will suffer greatly (Is 53:3-9). Many will reject Him, including His friends (Is 53:3-9).

He will be betrayed by a friend (Ps 41:9) for 30 pieces of silver (Zech 11:12,13). Later, that money will be thrown on the floor of the temple (Zech 11:12,13) and will eventually go to a potter (Zech 11:12,13). At His trial He will not defend Himself. He will say nothing (Is 53:3-9) except as required by law. Israel will reject Him (Is 8:14).

The Messiah will be taken to a mountaintop identified to Abraham as "the Lord will provide" (Gen 22). There He will be crucified with His hands and feet pierced (Ps 22). His enemies will encircle Him (Ps 22), mocking Him, and will cast lots for His clothing (Ps 22). He will call to God, asking why He was "forsaken" (Ps 22). He will be given gall and wine (Ps 69:20-22). He will die with thieves (Is 53:3-9). But, unlike the thieves, none of His bones will be broken (Ps 22). His heart will fail (Ps 22), as indicated by blood and water spilling out (Ps 22) when He is pierced with a spear (Zech 12:10). He will be buried in a rich man's grave (Is 53:3-9). In three days, He will rise from the dead (Ps 22).[103]

Are you yet convinced Jesus alone fulfills Old Testament prophecies that identify Him as Messiah—the Anointed One? The Bible establishes Jesus as Prophet, Priest, King, and Messiah. His many miracles, signs, and wonders fulfill hundreds of Old Testament prophecies.

Although many religious leaders have exalted themselves as gods, only the God of the Bible would lower Himself to become a man. His mission? Jesus was to lay His life down to pay for the sins of the entire world.[104]

---

[103] "AllAboutGOD.com Ministries, M. Houdmann, P. Matthews-Rose, R. Niles, editors, 2002-2014. Used by permission."

[104] See Philippians 2:7-9

Is Jesus Really God?

Many consider Jesus as a good man or a good teacher, but deny His divinity. A "good man" who declares Himself God would not be a good man or a good teacher; such a person would be a liar, a fraud, or a lunatic. He certainly wouldn't be a "good man."

Skeptics claim Jesus never said He was God, but Jesus' enemies knew better. They would ultimately succeed in killing Jesus for the crime of presenting Himself as Messiah.

Before we let Jesus' enemies enlighten our understanding, let's see what God the Father, the Apostles, and Jesus Himself said about Jesus' divinity.

Does God the Father Believe Jesus is God?

And a cloud came and overshadowed them; and a voice came out of the cloud, saying, 'This is My beloved Son. Hear Him!' (Mark 9:7)

But to the Son He [God the Father] says:
'Your throne, O God, is forever and ever;
A scepter of righteousness is the scepter of Your kingdom.'[105]
(Hebrews 1:8).

Did the Apostles Believe Jesus is God?

Now Jesus and His disciples went out to the towns of Caesarea Philippi; and on the road He asked His disciples, saying to them, 'Who do men say that I am?'
So they answered, 'John the Baptist; but some say, Elijah; and others, one of the prophets.'
He said to them, 'But who do you say that I am?'
Peter answered and said to Him, 'You are the Christ.'

---

[105] Also see Psalms 45:6-7.

Then He strictly warned them that they should tell no one about Him
(Mark 8:27-30).

In the beginning was the Word, and the Word was with God, and the Word was God. He was in the beginning with God. All things were made through Him, and without Him nothing was made (John 1:1-3).

He was clothed with a robe dipped in blood, and His name is called The Word of God. (Revelation 19:13)

And Thomas answered and said to Him, 'My Lord and my God!'
(John 20:28)

'Have this attitude in yourselves which was also in Christ Jesus, who, although He existed in the form of God, did not regard equality with God a thing to be grasped, but emptied Himself, taking the form of a bond-servant, and being made in the likeness of men. And being found in appearance as a man, He humbled Himself by becoming obedient to the point of death, even death on a cross.' (Phil. 2:5-8)

Did Jesus Claim to be God?

Jesus said to them, 'Most assuredly, I say to you, before Abraham was, I AM.' (John 8:58)

Then the Jews surrounded Him and said to Him, "How long do You keep us in doubt? If you are the Christ, tell us plainly." Jesus answered them, "I told you, and you do not believe. The works that I do in My Father's name, they bear witness of Me. But you do not believe, because you are not of My sheep, as I said to you, "My sheep hear My voice,

and I know them and they follow Me. And I give them eternal life, and they shall never perish; neither shall anyone snatch them out of My hand. My Father, who has given them to me, is greater than all; and no one is able to snatch them out of My Father's hand. I and My Father are one.
(John 10:24-30)

Jesus said to him, "Have I been with you so long, and yet you have not known Me, Philip? He who has seen Me has seen the Father; so how can you say, 'Show us the Father.' Do you not believe that I am in the Father, and the Father in Me? The words that I speak to you I do not speak on My own authority; but the Father who dwells in Me does the works. Believe Me that I am in the Father and the Father in Me, or else believe Me for the sake of the works themselves."
(John 14:9-11)

Then the devil took him to Jerusalem, to the highest point of the Temple, and said, "If you are the Son of God, jump off! For the Scriptures say,
'He will order his angels to protect and guard you.
And they will hold you up with their hands so you won't even hurt your foot on a stone'"
Jesus responded, "The Scriptures also say, 'You must not test the Lord your God.'"
(Luke 4:9-12)

Did Jesus' Enemies Understand Jesus Claimed to be God?

But Jesus answered them, 'My Father has been working until now, and I have been working.'
Therefore the Jews sought all the more to kill Him, because He not only broke the Sabbath, but also said that God was His Father, making Himself equal with God. (John 5:17-18)

84

*And the scribes and the Pharisees began to reason, saying,
'Who can forgive sins but God alone?' But when Jesus
perceived their thoughts, He answered and said to them,
'Why are you reasoning in your hearts? Which is easier to
say, 'your sins are forgiven you, or to say, 'Rise up and
walk?' But that you may know that the Son of Man has
power on earth to forgive sins,—He said to the man who
was paralyzed, 'I say to you, arise, take up your bed, and
go to your house.' Immediately, he rose up before them,
took up what he had been lying on, and departed to his own
house, glorifying God.* (Luke 5:21-25)

*The Jews answered Him, saying, 'For a good work we do
not stone You, but for blasphemy, and because You, being a
Man, make Yourself God.'*
(John 10:33)

*Now when the centurion, and they that were with him,
watching Jesus, saw the earthquake, and those things that
were done, they feared greatly, saying, 'Truly this was the
Son of God.'* (Matthew 27:54)

Most first-century audiences understood when Jesus claimed
"oneness" with His Father, He was equating Himself God. Today,
that terminology escapes many of us reading the passages in
English translations.

Also, through Exodus 34:14 God says: "For you shall not
worship any other God, for the LORD, whose name is Jealous, is
a jealous God."[106] If Jesus was not God, He sinned and violated
Exodus 34 by receiving worship in John 20:28, Hebrews 1:6,
Matthew 2:11, Matthew 8:2, Matthew 9:18, and John 9:38.

---

[106] New Living Translation

Jesus' divinity separates biblical Christianity from most world religions and nearly every Christian cult.

If Jesus were merely human, His imperfections would disqualify Him as the perfect, sinless sacrifice God required to cover our sins.

Animal sacrifices in the Old Testament foreshadowed Jesus' sacrifice. Many Jews traveled great distances to celebrate the required Passover feast. The Law required each Jewish family to bring (or purchase) an innocent, perfect lamb. During Passover, priests examined each lamb to ensure the lamb possessed no blemishes or imperfections. The approved lambs were killed and sacrificed as atonement for the sins of the people.

As the Passover lambs were being examined, Jesus as the Lamb of God was also being "examined" by various Jewish and Roman officials. Pilate as Jesus' final inspector said, "I find no fault in this man." Pilate then tried to release Jesus but he succumbed to political pressure.

As blood drained from Israel's sacrificial lambs, Roman soldiers flogged and crucified the Lamb of God and caused His blood to pour out.

Roman scourging victims often died. Jesus was not so fortunate. He not only endured the flesh ripping from His back, but willingly accepted the pain and shame of the cross to save the world from its sins.

During His interrogations, Jesus remained silent and would not defend Himself. Jesus died among wicked men, but they buried Him in a rich man's tomb. Isaiah, in another prophecy, recorded these details over seven hundred years earlier.

He was oppressed and He was afflicted,
Yet He opened not His mouth;
He was led as a lamb to the slaughter,
And as a sheep before its shearers is silent,
So He opened not His mouth.
He was taken from prison and from judgment,
And who will declare His generation?

For He was cut off from the land of the living;
For the transgressions of My people He was stricken.
And they made His grave with the wicked—
But with the rich at His death,
Because He had done no violence,
Nor was any deceit in His mouth.[107]

Similarly, Psalm 22 describes Jesus' thirst, His pierced hands and feet, and soldiers gambling for his garments.

My strength is dried up like a potsherd,
And My tongue clings to My jaws;
You have brought Me to the dust of death.
For dogs have surrounded Me;
The congregation of the wicked has enclosed Me.
They pierced My hands and My feet;
I can count all My bones.
They look and stare at Me.
They divide My garments among them,
And for My clothing they cast lots.[108]

Does the most supernatural sacrifice of the universe sound foolish? The Bible teaches that we will view the cross as foolishness or the power of God; our opinions depend upon whether or not we are "perishing."

For the message of the cross is foolishness to those who are perishing, but to us who are being saved it is the power of God.[109]

Receiving Jesus' sacrifice differs dramatically from putting merely attending church on Sunday and sprinkling in a few good

---

[107] Isaiah 53:7-9

[108] Psalm 22:15-18

[109] 1 Corinthians 1:18

works to try to earn salvation. Why settle for religion when we could know the King? Religions often impose odd restrictions that prohibit touching or handling certain "sacred" religious objects. Religions and their traditions compel us to obey the commandments and doctrines of men. Religious restrictions and activities sound wise but offer no power for transforming our flesh.

Religious conditioning creates mental caricatures of Christ that camouflage the Living, Resurrected Jesus with artificial philosophies and theologies.

The Jesus Christ of the Bible is Messiah, Savior, Prophet, Priest, and God. Any other view of Jesus is likely a caricature we can shatter by studying the Scriptures themselves.

Most of the world feels its arrogant, bigoted, and narrow-minded to believe Jesus is the only way to God. Yet, God did not have to provide *any* way back to Himself. Therefore, the arrogant, bigoted, narrow-minded ones are those who reject His means of salvation.

If you are still uncertain about Jesus' divinity or have questions about His salvation, ask Him for the truth: He's always listening, and we do not have to go through any other mediators!

Chapter 8
When God Gets Personal

Therefore, if anyone is in Christ, he is a new creation; old things have passed away; behold, all things have become new. (2 Corinthians 5:17)

Eddie filled a syringe as his bright-eyed, two-year-old daughter, anticipated daddy's next steps. After watching her father prepare his heroin, she ran into his bedroom to find something to help him tie up his arm before he injected the heroin. She skipped back into the living room with a beaming smile and a heroin tourniquet—the same tie Eddie usually wore to church on Sunday.

He glanced from his church necktie to his daughter's smile, and then back to the waiting syringe. Eddie's hypocrisy and the consequences of his addiction confronted him.

"Things were falling apart all around me," Eddie explained, "then, I ended up in prison. When I got out, I was still doing dope. Or I should say dope was doing me. One day while I was walking down the street trying to hustle money for my next fix, I looked down and saw a key chain tag on the sidewalk that read, 'Have not I commanded you? Be strong and of good courage: be not afraid, neither be you dismayed; for the LORD your God is with you wherever you go.'[110]

On October 20, 2000, Eddie promised God he would never shoot heroin again. He asked God to use him for His purposes. Eddie reflects, "It hasn't been easy. It's been a battle at times, but God has been faithful. He's done a miracle in my life."[111]

---

[110] From Isaiah 41:10

[111] A testimony from a former student named Eddie.

Has God done a miracle in your life? Church attendance failed to heal Eddie's hurt, anger, and bitterness. However, once Eddie surrendered his life to Jesus, old things passed away, and all things became new. Have all things become new for you?

Many do not battle addictions like Eddie did, but even many church-going people seem to struggle to find life's meaning and purpose. People seem to compensate for missing purpose by either becoming more religious or more worldly. Jesus wants us to know *Him*.

Our Gracious God

The Bible shows in many ways we can't satisfy God by trying to earn our salvation, doing good works, or keeping the Ten Commandments. Although it only takes one sin to disqualify us from eternal life, Christ compensates for all of our sins and reconciles us with God—if we will let Him.

> *For by grace you have been saved through faith; and that not of yourselves, it is the gift of God; not as a result of works, so that no one may boast. For we are His workmanship, created in Christ Jesus for good works, which God prepared beforehand so that we would walk in them.*[112]

This passage should purge us of any false notions of our works causing salvation. God's good works will start flowing through us once we receive Christ, but they do not cause us to be right with God. Although good works do not *cause* salvation, once we are reborn, we do them *because* of salvation.

Many religions falsely teach that if we clean up our acts, pursue their doctrines, participate in their rituals, and perform enough good works, we merit Heaven.

[112] Ephesians 2:8-10

Biblical Christianity teaches us that we can't attain salvation except through Jesus' sacrifice on the cross. Furthermore, we can't add to, or enhance, Jesus' perfect sacrifice. When Jesus said, "It is finished,"[113] I believe He meant it.

Although good works do not cause salvation, once we are reborn, we do them *because* of salvation.

Jesus clarifies the confusion about salvation to a religious Pharisee who knew he was missing something with his religion.

Nicodemus came to Jesus at night and asked a surprising question for a religious leader, "What must I do to be saved?"

Jesus answered, "You must be born again, or you cannot see the Kingdom of God."[114] Nicodemus understood *born again* as reentering his mother's womb. Jesus corrected Nicodemus' misunderstanding:

> *"I assure you, no one can enter the Kingdom of God without being born of water and the Spirit. Humans can reproduce only human life, but the Holy Spirit gives birth to spiritual life. So don't be surprised when I say, 'You must be born again.' The wind blows wherever it wants. Just as you can hear the wind but can't tell where it comes from or where it is going, so you can't explain how people are born of the Spirit."[115]*

Baptism identifies us with Jesus' burial and our "deadness" to sin's hold on us. Baptism is an external sign of what is supposed to be an internal transformation. Without an internal transformation, baptism merely provides warm, fuzzy, false assurances about our standing with the God of the Bible.

---

[113] John 19:30

[114] See John 3

[115] John 3:5-8, NLT

Many religious systems use baptism as a futile attempt to certify people as "saved." Although many church members haven't surrendered their hearts to God, they falsely believe their denomination's baptism rituals will bridge them into Heaven.

What have you been taught about baptism—does it *cause* change or does it *symbolize* change? The Bible clarifies baptism as a two-pronged symbol that identifies us with Jesus' death, but also His resurrection.

Or do you not know that as many of us as were baptized into Christ Jesus were baptized into His death?
Therefore we were buried with Him through baptism into death, that just as Christ was raised from the dead by the glory of the Father, even so we also should walk in newness of life[116]

If we're not walking in the newness of life, we may not have been born of the Spirit.

Religion often misapplies the biblical meaning of baptism. Jesus was baptized as an adult, but some denominations do not follow his example. An infant, for example, can't choose Christ or identify with Christ's death, burial, or resurrection. However, many churches baptize infants, assuring the parents their child just entered into eternal salvation. Although the Bible endorses water baptism as an important symbol, in practice, the internal change baptism symbolizes has often been lost.

In another example, as Jesus died between two thieves, the "bad thief" chided Jesus and said, "If You are the Christ, save Yourself and us."

The "good thief" rebuked him and said, "Do you not even fear God, seeing you are under the same condemnation? And we indeed justly, for we receive the due reward of our deeds; but this Man has done nothing wrong." Then the good thief said to Jesus, "Lord, remember me when You come into Your kingdom."[117]

---

[116] Romans 6:3-4

[117] See Luke 23:39-43

Jesus rewarded the good thief's faith by saying, "Today you will be with me in Paradise." [118]

This good thief received Jesus without baptism. He acknowledged his guilt, and sin, recognized Jesus as King, and put his life in Jesus' hands. He received the Gospel of Salvation. Paul states the Gospel:

> *By which also you are saved, if you keep in memory what I preached to you so that you haven't believed in vain. For I delivered to you that which I also received, how that Christ died for our sins according to the scriptures, and that he was buried, and that he rose again the third day according to the scriptures. And that he was seen of Cephas, then of the twelve, After that he was seen of about five hundred brethren at once, of whom the majority are alive today although some have died.[119]*

Although the good thief didn't witness Jesus' Resurrection, he understood who Jesus was, acknowledged his sin, and entered into a personal relationship with his Savior.

Since we've all sinned and fallen short of God's glory, we must receive the salvation Jesus freely provides for each of us.

If you haven't surrendered your heart to God, but want to do so, you can use the following prayer as a starting point as you call out to God in your own words. Thank Him for dying for your sins, and surrender your life to Him.

> *Lord Jesus, I receive you by faith with my heart and desire to make you the Lord of my life. Although I've sinned many times, You suffered and died on the cross to pay for each of them. I receive your sacrifice now for each of my sins. As I surrender my life to you, make*

---

[118] See Luke 23:44

[119] 1 Corinthians 15:2-8

yourself real to me. Open my heart, mind, soul, and
spirit so that I may hear and obey you. Amen.

Spiritual Seed and Spiritual Fruit

The Apostle Paul, the "good thief," and Eddie experienced dramatic transformations as they encountered Jesus, the Living Word of God.[120]

God's Word is also likened to sown seeds to further God's spiritual kingdom.[121] *Shattering the Stained Glass Jesus* attempted to extract some key seeds from the Word of God for your consideration. Prayerfully research these verses in your Bible and ask the Holy Spirit to reveal the truth—including any areas of spiritual deception.

Once God's seed (the truths of His Word) are planted into your heart, safeguard and nurture that seed through prayer and additional Bible study. Why?

Luke 8 describes three perils that can come against *the seed:*

The seed is the word of God. Those by the wayside are the ones who hear; then the devil comes and takes away the word out of their hearts, lest they should believe and be saved. But the ones on the rock are those who, when they hear, receive the word with joy; and these have no root, who believe for a while and in time of temptation fall away. Now the ones that fell among thorns are those who, when they have heard, go out and are choked with cares, riches, and pleasures of life, and bring no fruit to maturity. But the ones that fell on the good ground are those who, having heard the word with a noble and good heart, keep it and bear fruit with patience.[122]

---

[120] See Revelation 19:13

[121] See Luke 8:11

[122] Luke 8:12-18

If we nurture the seed with "noble and good hearts," we will bear spiritual fruit. Has the spiritual seed in your life produced positive fruit? "The fruit of the spirit is love, joy, peace, long suffering, kindness, goodness, faithfulness, gentleness, self-control. Against such there is no law."(Galatians 5:22-23).

Now contrast the Fruit of the Spirit with the *works of the flesh.*

> *Now the works of the flesh are evident, which are:*
> *adultery, fornication, uncleanness, lewdness, idolatry,*
> *sorcery, hatred, contentions, jealousies, outbursts of*
> *wrath, selfish ambitions, dissensions, heresies, envy,*
> *murders, drunkenness, revelries, and the like; of which*
> *I tell you beforehand, just as I also told you in time*
> *past, that those who practice such things will not inherit*
> *the kingdom of God.* [123]

Committing any of these individual sins does not disqualify us from inheriting God's Kingdom; "practicing" these sins separates us from God's Kingdom.

Epilogue

The verses in *Shattering the Stained Glass Jesus* hopefully exposed and shattered any religious or cultural obstacles that may have been blocking, discoloring, or distorting God's True Light from you, the reader.

We used the statements in the true/false quiz to compare our beliefs about what we thought the Bible taught and what it actually teaches. We asked, *if we are wrong about what it doesn't take to go to Heaven, could we be mistaken about what it does take?*

Since so many church-going people are mistaken about Jesus' core Good News Message—His Gospel of Salvation. Our eternal destiny is shaped by one important distinction: have we entered into a personal relationship with the Living Christ, or have we inherited an impersonal religious system.

---

[123] Galatians 5:19-21

In Chapter Two we clarified what the Bible says the Gospel is, why we need it, and how to receive it.

Next, we understood that before we could say the Bible, or any other spiritual writings are true or not, we needed to understand truth itself. Chapter Three defined truth, separated it from belief, and illustrated the differences between relative and absolute truths.

Chapter Four expanded the notion of truth by looking at the interplay between truth and deception. We asked if truth did not exist, how else could we ever recognize lies? Without absolute truth, we would never be able to say, "I'm absolutely sure someone lied to me."

We may not like Jesus' opinion, or we may not believe it. Perhaps the more important question is, "Is the Jesus of the Bible telling the truth?"

In Chapter Five, we examined some unique features separating the Bible from any other spiritual writings. We noticed the crucial role prophecy plays as it uniquely authenticates the Bible as God's Word. Prophecy sets the Bible apart from any other spiritual writings in the detail, quantity and quality of biblical prophecy.

The Bible uniquely established Jesus' credentials in advance through hundreds of detailed prophecies.

Furthermore, the Bible is internally consistent, historically accurate, and prophetically significant. Forty prophetic authors penned sixty-six books and letters that dovetail perfectly with each other.

In Chapter Six, we examined how our personal, cultural, and religious experiences create caricatures of Christ. Caricatures of Christ diminish some of His characteristics and exaggerate others. These caricatures cause many to completely misunderstand the Gospel of Salvation.

Nothing distinguishes the biblical Jesus from the caricatures of Christ more than the fact that Jesus Christ said He was God, So, in Chapter Seven we explored how God the Father said Jesus was God, the disciples regarded Jesus as God, and even Jesus' enemies knew Jesus presented Himself as God (John 10:33).

We explored the fact that if Jesus was not God, He was an imperfect sacrifice and unable to pay for any our sins. We also examined some evidence of Jesus' resurrection that fulfilled prophecy and is corroborated by other literature of the first century.

If first century skeptics could have produced Jesus' dead body, Christianity would have died. Yet Jesus lived and arose from the dead—just as the Bible prophesied.

In this chapter, we opened with Eddie's transformed life as evidence of the unique work of the Gospel of Salvation. When the Gospel moves from our heads to our hearts, life blossoms with purpose, meaning, and significance. Superficial, ritualistic, manmade religious practices or "good" human effort can't transform lives.

Despite the overwhelming evidence for the supernatural, historical, biblical Jesus, many still reject Him.

If the verses in this book helped you shatter a stained glass religious Christ, and you received Him into your heart, you can also ask Him for help with your next steps.

Lord Jesus, thank you for my new eternal life in you. I submit myself to you as a living sacrifice—my life is yours to do with as you choose. Help me to hear your voice and guide me to the right church and surround me with people you have chosen to disciple me so that I will be strengthened in my walk with you. Send me people who will pray with me and will encourage me with your Word. Protect me from deception and strengthen me against sin and temptation. Help me separate truth from lies and lead me by your wisdom. Amen.

If you didn't receive Him, or still have questions or concerns, ask God to clarify the truth. Ask Jesus to reveal Himself to you. He loves you and wants to be with you for eternity.

True or False Quiz Answers for Chapter One

1) If I believe in God, I will go to Heaven.

The answer is false because there is more to attaining Heaven than merely believing in God's existence.

The Bible teaches, "You say you have faith, for you believe that there is one God. Good for you! Even the demons believe this, and they tremble in terror" (James 2:19, NLT). Demons and Satan believe God exists, but they will not spend eternity in Heaven.

The God of the Bible does not consider our belief in Him as such a great accomplishment. He makes Himself known through His creation:

They know the truth about God because he has made it obvious to them. For ever since the world was created, people have seen the earth and sky. Through everything God made, they can clearly see his invisible qualities—his eternal power and divine nature. So they have no excuse for not knowing God. Yes, they knew God, but they wouldn't worship him as God or even give him thanks. And they began to think up foolish ideas of what God was like. As a result, their minds became dark and confused. Claiming to be wise, they instead became utter fools. (Romans 1:19-22, NLT)

Chapter Two contains the verses that show you what the Bible teaches it takes for you to gain Heaven.

2) I will go to Heaven if I am a good person.

The answer is false because God does not attribute goodness to anyone but Jesus; only Jesus Christ as God is good (Luke 18:19).

Similarly, the God of the Bible does not consider our works good: *All have turned away, they have together become worthless, there is no one who does good, not even one* (Romans 3:10).

The Bible shows some who performed miracles and cast out demons in Jesus' name will be surprised when Jesus rejects them.

> *Many will say to Me in that day, 'Lord, Lord, have we not prophesied in Your name, cast out demons in Your name, and done many wonders in Your name?' And then I will declare to them, 'I never knew you; depart from Me, you who practice lawlessness!* (Matthew 7:22-23)

The God of the Bible demands a moral perfection we cannot attain without receiving Jesus' perfection. When we receive Him, we inherit His perfection. Jesus Christ as a Personal Savior differs from *the Stained Glass Jesus* of religion, personal beliefs, or spiritual experience.

3) If I keep the Ten Commandments, I'll go to Heaven.

This question is false because no one has kept the Ten Commandments except Jesus. Keeping some Commandments, some of the time, differs from perfectly obeying *all* of His Commandments *all* of the time.

According to the Bible, "whoever keeps the whole Law, and yet stumbles in just one point, is guilty of breaking the entire Law" (James 2:10). We break God's *entire law* if we break one commandment.

It's too late to earn Heaven by "keeping" the Ten Commandments. The Bible explains:

> *For the same God who said, 'You must not commit adultery,' also said, 'You must not murder.' So if you murder someone but do not commit adultery, you have still broken the law* (James 2:11 NLT).

The Law was not established to be "kept," but to highlight our hopelessness and point us toward our need for a savior, Jesus. The Bible clarifies the Law's purpose:

> *The law was our guardian until Christ came; it protected us until we could be made right with God through faith. And now that the way of faith has come, we no longer need the law as our guardian (Galatians 3:24-25).*

Chapter Two explains the Gospel and clarifies what the Bible says it takes to go to Heaven.

4) Many paths lead to God.

The answer is false because the Bible teaches there is only one path to God—one way. Jesus said, "I am the way, the truth, and the life, no one comes to the Father except through me" (John 14:6). Furthermore, the Bible teaches, *there is one God and one Mediator between God and men, the man Christ Jesus* (1 Timothy 2:5).

The Apostle Peter explained to those who crucified Jesus that salvation comes from only one Savior.

> *Let me clearly state to all of you and to all the people of Israel that he was healed by the powerful name of Jesus Christ the Nazarene, the man you crucified but whom God raised from the dead. For Jesus is the one referred to in the Scriptures, where it says,*
> *'The stone that you builders rejected*
> * has now become the cornerstone.'*
> *There is salvation in no one else! God has given no other name under heaven by which we must be saved. (Acts 4:10-12)*

5) Most people are good at heart.

According to the Bible, we each have deceitful and wicked hearts; the answer is false.

The Bible teaches that our hearts are incurably wicked (Jeremiah 17:9).

Similarly, the New Testament shows that only God can truly know our hearts through His Spirit.

The heart is deceitful above all things and beyond cure. Who can understand it? 'I the LORD search the heart and examine the mind, to reward a man according to his conduct, according to what his deeds deserve' (1 Corinthians 2:10-12).

Jesus describes distant hearts of hypocrites who worship Him with their mouths, but not their hearts.

Hypocrites! Well did Isaiah prophesy about you, saying:
'These people draw near to Me with their mouth,
And[a] honor Me with their lips,
But their heart is far from Me.
And in vain they worship Me,
Teaching as doctrines the commandments of men' (Matthew 15:7-9)

King David understood the condition of his heart and prayed,

Create in me a clean heart, O God,
And renew a steadfast spirit within me.
Do not cast me away from Your presence,
And do not take Your Holy Spirit from me. (Psalms 51:10-11)

According to Jesus, we can know the condition of someone's heart by listening to what they talk about. Jesus teaches us that from the abundance of our hearts, our mouths speak (Luke 6:43-45).

6) Most people will go to Heaven.

The answer is false because according to the Bible, *few* people inherit Heaven and *many* receive the Lake of Fire.

The Bible clearly teaches Jesus is the only way to God.

You can enter God's Kingdom only through the narrow gate. The highway to hell is broad, and its gate is wide for the many who choose that way. But the gateway to life is very narrow and the road is difficult, and only a few ever find it. (Matthew 7:13-14)

Although Jesus is the only way to God, and many say they have a solid relationship with Jesus, the Bible teaches many will be surprised when they appear before Him on Judgment Day.

> "Not everyone who calls out to me, 'Lord! Lord!' will enter the Kingdom of Heaven. Only those who actually do the will of my Father in heaven will enter. On Judgment Day many will say to me, 'Lord! Lord! We prophesied in your name and cast out demons in your name and performed many miracles in your name.' But I will reply, 'I never knew you. Get away from me, you who break God's laws'" (Matthew 7:21-23).

If demon-casting, wonder-working prophets who worked their miracles under the authority of Jesus' name could mistake Heaven for Hell, why couldn't we err? You don't have to make the same eternal mistake as miracle-workers; Chapter Two will show you what the Bible teaches about the Gospel of Salvation and how to receive Jesus (instead of religion).

7) God helps those who help themselves.

The answer is false: "God helps those who helps themselves" is not in the Bible. In fact, the Bible teaches we *can't help ourselves.*

Sin leaves each of us hopelessly lost (Romans 3:23) and condemned (Romans 6:23). We can't go to Heaven through our own efforts or with the help of religious rules and rituals that falsely appear to compensate for our sin or please God.

Since we can't remedy our sin situation (Isaiah 64:6), God devised a plan to redeem us. *While we were still sinners, Jesus died for us* (Romans 5:8). Jesus paid the penalty for sin that we couldn't pay (2 Corinthians 5:21). We need to surrender Our own efforts to help ourselves, but we can receive Jesus and His finished work on the cross.

8) Jesus was a good man but not God.

This statement is false because, accordion got the Bible, Jesus is God. God the Father calls His Son "God" and identifies Christ as laying the foundation of the earth and credits Jesus with making the heavens.

> But to the Son he says,
> 'Your throne, O God, endures forever and ever.
>   You rule with a scepter of justice.
> You love justice and hate evil.
>   Therefore, O God, your God has anointed you,
>   pouring out the oil of joy on you more than on anyone else.'
> He also says to the Son,
> 'In the beginning, Lord, you laid the foundation of the earth
>   and made the heavens with your hands.' (Hebrews 1:8-10, NLT)

The doubting Apostle, Thomas, also declared Jesus was God,

> And after eight days His disciples were again inside, and Thomas with them. Jesus came, the doors being shut, and stood in the midst, and said, "Peace to you!" Then He said to Thomas, "Reach your finger here, and look at My hands; and reach your hand here, and put it into My side. Do not be unbelieving, but believing."
> And Thomas answered and said to Him, 'My Lord and my God!' (John 20:26-28)

We dedicate Chapter Seven to the central question of Jesus' divinity.

9) Hell is not a literal place.

The answer is false because Hell is a literal place that blazes with eternal fire; Jesus warned extensively about it.

> But if you cause one of these little ones who trusts in me to fall into sin, it would be better for you to be thrown into the sea with a large millstone hung around your neck. If your hand causes you to sin, cut it off. It's better to enter eternal life with only one hand than to go into the unquenchable fires of hell with two hands. If your foot causes you

to sin, cut it off. It's better to enter eternal life with only one foot than to be thrown into hell with two feet. And if your eye causes you to sin, gouge it out. It's better to enter the Kingdom of God with only one eye than to have two eyes and be thrown into hell,'where the maggots never die and the fire never goes out. (Mark 9:42-48, NLT)

In another passage, a dead rich man describes his experience in Hell.

Jesus said,'There was a certain rich man who was splendidly clothed in purple and fine linen and who lived each day in luxury. At his gate lay a poor man named Lazarus who was covered with sores. As Lazarus lay there longing for scraps from the rich man's table, the dogs would come and lick his open sores.
Finally, the poor man died and was carried by the angels to be with Abraham. The rich man also died and was buried, and his soul went to the place of the dead. There, in torment, he saw Abraham in the far distance with Lazarus at his side.
The rich man shouted,'Father Abraham, have some pity! Send Lazarus over here to dip the tip of his finger in water and cool my tongue. I am in anguish in these flames.'
But Abraham said to him,'Son, remember that during your lifetime you had everything you wanted, and Lazarus had nothing. So now he is here being comforted, and you are in anguish. And besides, there is a great chasm separating us. No one can cross over to you from here, and no one can cross over to us from there.' (Luke 16:19-26, NLT)

Hell is real and only Jesus can deliver us from it. He teaches us to come to Him and receive His sacrifice.

10) We are all God's children.

The answer is false because we aren't God's children unless we meet His requirement. According to the God of the Bible, we must believe in Jesus and accept Him; then we qualify as one of His children.

He came into the very world he created, but the world didn't recognize him. He came to his own people, and even they rejected him. But to all who believed him and accepted him, he gave the right to become children of God. (John 1:10-12, NLT)

I must "believe Him and receive Him," if I want Him to consider me His child.

Proof

Made in the USA
Charleston, SC
23 December 2016